THE CARDINAL ANTHOLOGY VOL. 3

The Cardinal Anthology Vol. 3

H.S. LEIGH KOONCE, EDITOR

Ellerslie Books

CONTENTS

FOREWORD - xiii

Storm's A-Comin'
1

Homeless
2

Justice for a Nature
4

Violated Twice
5

My Queer Friend Tries to Tell Their Mother
7

Caged in Gaza
8

Now We Know
10

Callous Calluses
12

I Saw
14

Covid 2024

15

I Need A Virtue

16

Family dinner

18

the poet must be k!lled

19

The Fifth Wave

21

An Ode to a Cup of Tea

23

The Rules of Life

25

To Be Of Use

26

Octopus

27

the dreamer [the fires/ his paradise]

28

Unheard Cries

30

The Midwife's Tale

32

Let's Talk

49

ecdysis of green flowers

52

George and the Drag On

54

Folie À Deux

64

Trapped in Trepidation

66

They Didn't Care

67

The World is Upside Down // Il Mondo Alla Rovescia

69

When Indoctrination is A-OK

70

Bare Bones

71

Reflection: Can a Flame Freeze?

73

Blood on the Flag

74

Theft

76

There's Something
86

My Pipe Bomb Dream
88

Verily
90

This Aardvark
92

Extolling the Other Half
94

Voiceless
96

Every Word An Elegy
97

Social Justice against Gender Disparity
100

The Pool
114

Coopers Rock-Man
123

Charumbira, It's a Nude and Notorious Genocide
125

Justice for the People
128

Apparitions

130

In America

145

Strange world

147

inaleinable

148

Nature Nurtures Unconditionally

149

Exodus

150

Jamie

151

Social Justice

152

Another Title for Boys in the Cemetery

153

Rerouting

154

You Will Have to Cope With It As If It's Standard or Superlative

156

Befriend the Purple Man

158

x ~ *Contents*

A Forest's Last Whisper

160

Your State Can Protect You from Your Own Choices

162

Edges

163

Follow the Leader

165

She

167

Jintishi Poem for the Pandemic Winters

168

The Red Wine Sparkles as Gammadion Burns

170

Casualties

172

Layoff

174

Not Burnt Out Yet!!!

176

The Curse

177

If We Do Nothing

180

The red-white-red flag
181

Night syndrome
182

pilgrim of survival
183

Plastic Applicator
186

Silent Witness
188

The Retraction of Rights
190

Mary Tells How It Was and Will Ever Be
192

The Sirens of the Pylons
194

All Gone
196

Same place
197

Poem for Chess
198

The Rain for Gaza
200

10 Seconds to Live

202

In the Name of God

207

the bomb, not a bomb, the a bomb

209

CONTRIBUTORS - 211

FOREWORD

Foreword

The Cardinal Anthology was launched as a small, social justice oriented publication in late 2022. Our first issue mainly included folks around my geographic area in the Eastern Panhandle of West Virginia in the United States. In the span of a year and a half, we've grown. Though we are still a small publication, I'm proud to report geographically our contributors cover five continents, North America, Asia, Africa, Europe, and Australia. Our third edition also features more individual submissions than we've ever had.

I'm pleased to share this information because it demonstrates that an interest in social justice, as well as economic, reproductive, and environmental justice, is alive and well and exists across demographics and, indeed, oceans.

I hope you, the readers, will feel inspired to take action for your favorite cause after delving into the work featured in this edition.

My best,

Leigh Koonce, Editor & Publisher

PS. Please note some submissions in this edition are from non-native English speakers and those residing in countries in which English is not the dominant language. Therefore, some pieces utilize English in a form that may not be of the standard usage certain readers recognize. Please do not assume this is a lack of editing; rather it is the practice of the authors using English to tell their stories.

STORM'S A-COMIN'

Andi Stout

A bitter squall rips through
the mountain chain, shaking
snow off pine branches,
piercing the warmth of her
winter lined wool coat.
She loads Christmas gifts
she managed to pay off
just in the nick of time
on 12 weeks of layaway
into her pre-owned Chevy,
leaving an empty shopping cart
parked between yellow lines
of a neighboring space,
hoping to beat the storm
she can already smell coming.

HOMELESS

Melanie Flores

Winter blusters in early this year,
bitter, cold, and austere.
He pushes his shopping cart from bin to bin -
empty wine bottles and beer cans,
leftover pasta in takeout containers,
a threadbare child's blanket
with faded pink and yellow puppies -
voraciously collected.

Holiday decorations brighten the nights,
sounds of festivity and colourful lights.
He pushes his shopping cart from house to house -
glimpses of children through veiled windows,
elicit memories - a boy and a girl,
the touch of a feminine hand,
a house of laughter and warmth -
long gone, merely faded shadows.

A new year heralds promise and hope,
but not for a soul too broken to cope.
He pushes his thoughts from memory to memory -
gnarled fingers, toes frozen in place,
a furious fever gnaws at his body

as the cherished puppy blanket,
does little to keep in the warmth -
and his heart slows to an abrupt... halt.

JUSTICE FOR A NATURE

Binod Dawadi

Who will love nature ?
All are selfish and materialistic,
All want wealth they don't see,
Any destruction in the nature,
They are building a big houses,
As well as big apartments,
They are developing infrastructure of development,
But when they will love and care nature,

When will they listen,
To a marginal voices of the nature ?
Nature is crying and shouting,
Fighting for it's justice,
But human beings never listens to it,
Nature is a God which is,
Our home nature is our mother,
Who loves and cares for forever.

VIOLATED TWICE

Vanessa Caraveo

The surgery I had been dreading
no longer awaits ahead,
but instead of being thrilled,
I wonder if I'm dead.

Dead as I lay here, afraid
that I will be a sacrifice
for a child that no one wants.

Its father is a drug-fueled rapist
who now sits behind bars.
Its mother will die upon conception,
rejoining the sun and stars.

I dreaded it. Choosing myself
over this tiny life inside me.
But my body cannot set it free.

The odds of the baby's survival slim
and mine worse still than that.
But now I'm forced to conceive,
at the tip of a judge's hat.

Raped twice in such short succession.
Once by a man, once by a system.
No semblance of autonomy.

Doctors and nurses shuffle quietly.
They know how to save me.
But in the so-called greatest country,
we can never hope to be free.

One step forward, two steps back
leaves some innocents to die.
But the gears turn anyway.
A machine cannot cry.

Leave that to my family,
desperately begging to save me
from the footsteps of a country
that has once again raped me.

MY QUEER FRIEND TRIES TO
TELL THEIR MOTHER

Cecil Morris

In heaven we will all be ungendered, unclothed, too,
our bodies dissolved, all of us the same bright color,
a shimmer, if you will, so many leaves on a tree
of light, or motes by radiance defined and floating,
the substance of soul refined and clarified at last,
the dust of stars released by God's accepting love.

CAGED IN GAZA

Lynn White

She asked me why caged birds sang.
I couldn't tell her,
not for sure.
No mate will arrive this year,
and no freedom will come.
I wonder if they remember freedom,
perhaps they still
live in hope
like us.

She asked me if they felt fear as we do
when they heard the bombs falling.
I couldn't tell her,
not for sure.
I wonder if they remember peace,
Perhaps it will arrive this year,
unlike last year.
perhaps they still
live in hope
like us.

She asked me if they knew
they brought us comfort.

"I think that's why
they still sing,
like us,"
I said.

NOW WE KNOW

Corey-Jan Albert

The rise to anger, violence, riot, terror build up slow
through bold affronts to race, identity, belief, fertility, appearance.
For so long, I have asked, "Where is the outrage?" Now we know

it grew from seeds of doubt, imagined threats, of friend or foe,
as if what makes one greater, lesser, stemmed from some inherence.
The rise to anger, violence, riot, terror build up slow

transforming "us" into "us versus them," distrust, resentment grow
until the fear felt in the brain, heart, bones take on new
   incoherence.
For so long, I have asked, "Where is the outrage?" Now we know

it comes with human dignity ignored, run over, crushed below
the feet of those who see their God-granted supremacy's
   disappearance.
The rise to anger, violence, riot, terror build up slow

with salves of education, fortune, wellness torn down low
by fire hoses, tear gas, boots, rewards for measured perseverance.
For so long, I have asked, "Where is the outrage?" Now, we know

the answer to the question of the depths to which we'll go:
There is no bottom. Yet civility and deference demand adherence.

The rise to anger, violence, riot, terror build up slow
For so long, I have asked, "Where is the outrage?" Now, we know.

CALLOUS CALLUSES

Liam Kerry

In fresh skin, I met them,
And prayed they made it quick.
They ripped it from my body,
So it could grow back thick.

They taught me how to posture,
To fight and how to stand,
To throw insults and punches,
With my new, padded hands.

The skin kept growing denser,
Pulled tight, it couldn't hold.
The cracks were patched with Carbon,
Set inside their mold.

Held inside, imprisoned,
Trapped with screams and wails,
Emotions can't find freedom,
Held tight by leather scales,

Fresh-faced, fresh-skinned, he enters,
Happy, free and new,
Something seems familiar,
The old me in you?

Together we stand, mirrored,
His smile mocks my frown,
His skin, pristine and perfect,
I have to take him down.

I SAW

Adriana Rocha

Her skin was dark,
she had a child,
she was scared,
keeping her face down,
hiding it between her shoulders,
even though she was
tall, she was
attempting to
be small.
What I saw,
broke my heart,
I was screaming inside,
it was a mother surviving
a violent world.

COVID 2024

Allan Lake

Stolen delivery van
left abandoned in my throat
set on fire

I NEED A VIRTUE

Marieta Maglas

It's true for me if I believe it.

I may believe it, but it may be wrong.

It might be a lie.

So, I may believe something wrong

I can refuse to believe it, but it can be right.

There's no right or wrong,

Or there is no truth for me.

Anyway, I must believe in something.

So, I need a virtue.

I need the truth.

Now, all I know is that I have a need.

Can anyone tell me

Because I need to know,

'Can a virtue be taught? '

'Can a virtue be taught? '

FAMILY DINNER

Christopher T. Dabrowski
Julia Mraczny, Trans.

As I do every week, I put on my mediumistic amplifier helmet - we all have a predisposition to it, but most don't develop it.

Grandparents and parents are at the table.

Only the great-grandparents are missing. They decided to have another incarnation.

We eat an ectoplasmic dinner.

- I am dying, I declare. - I have an incurable...

Everyone rejoices.

- But I stay for the children.

- Son, what do you mean...

- I can't do otherwise. I've just set up a dropbox android with possession feature. I'll have to raise money for a subscription...

- We respect your decision - father breaks the awkward silence.

THE POET MUST BE K!LLED

Joseph E. Arechavala

the poet must be k!lled
poetry is dangerous
seductive, divisive, seditious
poetry blasphemes
defiles, decries, defies, despises
decolonizes its subjects
denigrates our traditions
poetry is the wrecking ball
to societal norms
poetry is dangerous
so dangerous
do you understand?
it lies in wait
reminds us the supernatural and
mystic are only fools on stage
poetry is degenerate
the poet must be k!lled
because they know words matter
and think truth dies
with them the poet must be k!lled
the poet must be k!lled
poetry is dangerous
seductive, divisive, seditious

poetry blasphemes
defiles, decries, defies, despises
decolonizes its subjects
denigrates our traditions
poetry is the wrecking ball
to societal norms
poetry is dangerous
so dangerous
do you understand?
it lies in wait
reminds us the supernatural and
mystic are only fools on stage
poetry is degenerate
the poet must be k!lled
because they know words matter
and think truth dies
with them

THE FIFTH WAVE

Dotty LeMieux

1.

Or is it the sixth?
This one we ride out
in silence
Accept eight new tests
from the government
Biden tests
Accept $1500 from the US Treasury,
consolation prize

2.

So far, knock on wood, we haven't gotten sick
Funny word, gotten, like given,
only from the receiver's point of view
As children, we got reprimanded
if we used that bastard word
When did it become acceptable, unavoidable?
Maybe about the time they stopped letting kids
get childhood diseases.
When I was young, they even sent you
over to a sick kid's house,

"Get the measles," they'd say,
and get it over with

3.

I have gotten over with COVID,
but it hasn't gotten over with me
So I wear the mask, & carry the vaccine card
everywhere, badge of honor,
like a tin badge on a tv sheriff,
a flimsy thing which may not provide
protection against sneaky mutating germs.
Today we passed the one million mark,
one million deaths from this disease
and how many more
have got it, but live, inoculated
by their exposure,
but not, we know now,
ever gotten over it.

AN ODE TO A CUP OF TEA

Mohammad Haseen Ahmed

Being most of my life a non-smoker and teetotaler I easily fell
    prey to the
aroma of first and then next and after tea and find myself utterly
    hooked and
enslaved till today.
A victim or a Victor for a loner like me everyday
Keep sniffing and coming to life afresh
Unmindful of the woes and the digress,
Life would be impossible to relish
Tea helps me reminisce and regale
Without it perhaps I would perish and pester
Thanks to the Britishers, our coloniser
Who left us a bit enriched with the grandeur
This brewing helps kill many feuds
Friends or foes, treats them alike
Fostering a lasting bond during the sipping
No wonder we have its ceremonies to celebrate
All of us deliberate to prove its efficacy,
In celibacy or in pure delicacy ,
I often wonder ! Would the world be the same in agonies and pain
    without this
panacea in plain, black or green with milk or without
I can vouch for its serenity without doubt!

Keep drinking this nectar
Spreading the message of its cementing force
To unite the humanity in anguish and woes
Forget all your ailments and pain
Stay alive and nudge out of your slumber
Slowly waking up the worldly wonders!

THE RULES OF LIFE

Anna Judit Hegedus

Nothing in this world can take your smile away
Nothing on the Earth **can** set you limits today
Don't let people **control** your feelings
Just do what your heart beats for and is good for **you**!
Do not want **more**
Than you really need, let your mind be the only compass that
    leads.
Live for **your** happiness but remember that your real happiness
    isn't terrestrial
Beyond death there's nothing left to **own**
Even your **thoughts** will be shown...

TO BE OF USE

Rob Rolfe

(Part of *Gaza Poems*)

i can not sleep
as kids die in gaza

i ask myself
of what use are

the words of a poet
already at fault

for loving too much
or too little

OCTOPUS

Natalie Fraser

Eight-legged sea creature
soft little shape-shifter
such a strange beauty,
tentacles and curls.

Trapped in a tiny tank
with gawking, jeering faces
tortuous monotony– she plans her escape.

Out, across the floor,
to a miniscule drainpipe
persisting two hundred feet
until she reaches the sea.

Cheer her brave escape,
her release from suffering
cheer for liberty
for all living beings.

THE DREAMER [THE FIRES/ HIS PARADISE]

Emmanuel Umeji

In the eyes of every dreamer, a paradise breathes—
I mean every dreamer is just another lost bird rooting for routes
     to its nest.

we're testaments to how this journey kickstarted:
how one day, reality stole your kickstands watching to see you
     stand like /
as a bicycle. how it peeled you naked like a banana set for
     teeth-work, watching
you as you face winter in the face.

how it cease your heater on a harmattan day, made bathing
     mandatory as breathing
& the options it dropped close to your skin are:
snow-water bath//snow-water bath// snow-water bath// aborting
your breath//

we're testaments to where the journey keeps spinning like a
     carousel—
on your study desk as nights watch you awake, burning a sackful
     of suns

over carving out a paradise from plane pages. how on that freaking
    evening in the cab,
after wrestling with the day for a pinch of time
to remind your neck about pillow, your phone beamed,
alarming you that you still have a pin to find in a haystack.
you sighed. you almost raise hands to life.

here is where the journey blends into crumbs digestible by men:
of the moment you walked into the mouth of a shark,
 watching its teeth entrap you in like Jericho Walls.
of the days you spent in here that tastes like fire & hunger.
of the countless seconds you almost succumbed
to the thought of draining your dreams
from your palms. of the fat minutes it took you to not let hope
    drown in the turbulence.
of how at last, the journey clinks flute with you;
you finally taste paradise, like Jonah.
Oases blooming in your desert, like Noah, like Noah.

UNHEARD CRIES

Magnolia Silcox

No one is there to hear her cries

As she lays down in pain and slowly dies

They said that Roe v. Wade was overturned to protect a life

But who's protecting her as she feels like she is being stabbed in the gut by a knife

No one cares if she has been raped

No one cares if she was sex trafficked and sold while her mouth is gaged and duct taped

No one gives a damn if it was incest

The cops are coming to put her under arrest

No one cares if the fertilized egg inside is slowly killing her

A child being forced to have another child with things never being able to go back to the way they were

Young girls asked uncomfortable questions about their monthly periods

Religious leaders counting a woman's choice as one of many sins

Old men voting on what happens to a woman's body when they haven't got a clue

A woman's body doesn't work the same as there's do

Young girls and women no longer free

They scream and cry because men won't just let them be

Being jailed for having a miscarriage

They could be detained at any age

Is a female's life so worthless that we are left for dead

Shouldn't our healthcare needs be valued instead

In this day and age a woman's cries are unheard

As we are left for dead in this cruel unforgiving world

THE MIDWIFE'S TALE

Cathy LaForge Tonkin

This story is about Margaret Finnegan Donnovan Foley. Margaret, who was called Maggie, was quite a formidable woman. She was a great lady and her life was impressive. Some of her acquaintances were a bit frightened of her because Maggie knew secrets about most everyone in town. And she kept these secrets taking them to her grave they say.

Maggie Finnegan was born on January 19, 1828, in Castlemaine, Kerry County, Ireland, the daughter of Catherine Sullivan and Jeremiah Finnegan. Her mother died when she was just 12 years old of heart failure. Catherine had been born with a weak heart and it had finally given out in 1840. Young Maggie was in shock and unable to function very well, spending most of her time in bed crying. Jerry was at a loss as to how to help his daughter. Catherine had always been the one who dealt with Maggie's issues. Now Jerry was left with 2 children and still trying to make plans to move to America.

Jerry Finnegan was a full blooded Irishman born in Killarnay, in County Kerry on February 5, 1779 and was a lifelong farmer. He married Catherine Sullivan in 1804 in Killarney and they had a son, John, born on June 5, 1825. Their daughter, Maggie, was born on January 19, 1828 in Castlemaine.

Being a farmer in Ireland back then was very tough work. The land was rocky and the climate was damp so not very conducive to raising crops. He thought that he would have a better chance of making a living in the U.S.

Jerry and his children carried on with their plan to emigrate to the U.S. They arrived in 1847 when Maggie was 19 years old and John was 22. She was the first white women to settle in the upper peninsula of Michigan at Eagle Harbor. It was there that she met Timothy Donovan.

Tim was born in 1820 in Cork, Ireland. He left that country to go to the U.S. where he found work as a carpenter. His skills were in demand because all areas of society benefitted from the work of carpenters as new houses and commercial buildings were being constructed all over the country. New housing was needed for the influx of immigrants arriving from all over Europe.

Maggie and Tim met at church. Her father knew Tim from church and thought he was a stand up guy so he was happy when the two hit it off. They courted for a little over a year then she married Timothy Donovan on August 22, 1847 in Chippewa County, Sault St. Marie, Michigan when he was 27 and she was 18. They had one daughter, Catherine born the following year.

He died as a young father in 1851 at the age of 31. Tim worked at the Forest Mine, near Ontonogan, Michigan. There was a cave in that killed him while he was down in the mine and 4 other men also met their maker on that day. Tim was taken by boat from Houghton, Michigan to Sault St. Marie where he is buried. His daughter was just 3 years old when he died and she would have no memory of him.

Maggie raised her little girl on her own, depending on her father, Jerry, and her brother John for their help and support. The four of them would attend services each Sunday at St. Mary's Catholic church.

This is when she started treating family and friends health problems. She learned to be a healer from a very old woman who she met with almost daily to learn the healers skills.

Martha Willows was a very wise old woman that Maggie respected and thought very highly of. She taught her the many types of herbs and tinctures to help with patients illnesses. She was also a midwife and Maggie learned all the ins and outs of childbirth.

It was at a church social that Maggie met James Foley. He had a never ending smile and the charm to go with it and he really turned on the charm for Maggie. She fell for him in a big way. Jerry liked Jim but the 2 were moving way too fast he thought. James was a mine owner and had worked in that field for many years.

Maggie married Captain James F. Foley in 1854 and they set up home in a nice little rental cottage on a dead end street in Negaunee. The 2 happy newlyweds spent their first week of marriage planning where they would eventually settle. Maggie had always seen herself in bigger city with a bigger family but it wasn't to be. She felt that James was ensconced in the town and wouldn't want to leave. His mine was nearby and he probably wouldn't want to live too much further from work.

The Captain achieved his rank after he enlisted in the Union Army, Company "C," 10th Minnesota Infantry. Company "C" mustered in October 7, 1861. Their last action was the Battle of Bentonville from March 19 to the 21st, 1865. The 2nd Minnesota Infantry mustered out of service in July of 1865.

Maggie's brother, John Finnegan, died in the civil war on June 27, 1862 at the Battle of Gaines Mills County, Iowa. He had fought with honor and was issued the purple heart posthumously.

She, as an experienced midwife, relied on the practical experience she got in delivering many children. As a skilled midwife she was highly valued. Other communities tried to attract her to their town by offering a higher salary and a rent-free house. She was flattered by their offer but she wasn't going to leave her town. She was very happy there and cared for her friends and neighbors. And they cared for her. They would often bring her a pie or a cake as a thank you for taking such good care of them.

Maggie enjoyed living in a small town because of the slower pace of life, family-oriented events, walkability and a being near nature. Science shows that living in small towns is beneficial for both your physical and your mental health. There is also a study that states people who live in areas with lots of trees and greenery can live longer than people in urban areas.

After they had been married for about eight months, Maggie found that she was expecting a baby. She hadn't wanted this to happen for another year or so but there she was. Their son, David, was born in March of 1855 and was a beautiful bald headed boy.

James was thrilled to have a son. He felt his life was complete. A great career, a wonderful wife and now a son. He couldn't have been happier. Maggie could. But she told herself she had to quit dreaming and be happy with the way her life had turned out.

James bought them a house when David was seven months old. It was a handsome four square with 3 bedroom and indoor plumbing.

Maggie was happy but also felt she had missed out on her chance for a bigger more important life.

The Foleys eventually had three children together, David, Pryor born in 1857, and daughter Mary Margaret, born in 1860.

Perie died after suffering with stomach cancer which caused indescribable pain. His illness started out with indigestion, abdominal pain, nausea, and vomiting. His illness progresses to vomiting blood, loss of appetite, weight loss and fatigue. It was almost a relief when he died. His family didn't want him to suffer any longer.

He had been a quiet man and well known as patient and kind and he would be greatly mourned by his family. Maggie was totally bereft when he died and didn't know how to go on. She still had Catherine, David and Mary so she tried to comfort herself by taking care of them.

These children eventually married and had families of their own. Maggie was always on hand to watch her grandchildren when ever their parents needed a break. She loved spoiling them, always having candy and cookies on hand. But every day she thought of Perry and how she missed him.

Maggie liked to tell her grandchildren stories from her long life. Their favorite was The Great Blizzard of 1888, also known as the Great White Hurricane. It blew from March 11 to the 14, 1888. It was one of the most severe recorded blizzards in American history. The storm paralyzed a great swath of the country.

Snow fell from 10 to 58 inches in parts and had winds of more than 45 miles per hour and produced snow drifts of more than 50 feet high. Maggie was living in Negaunee, Michigan at that time and was totally snowed in at her home. There were reports of drifts covering three-story houses. Jim had to dig a tunnel out the front door for them to be able to leave the house but even then they couldn't go anywhere because the main streets were not cleared.

Neither rail nor road travel was possible anywhere for days, and drifts across the main rail line took eight days to clear. Also, telegraph lines were down, isolating large parts of the midwest and most of the northeastern cities from Washington, D.C. to Boston for days. Fire stations were immobilized, and property loss from fires alone was estimated at $25 million.

More than 400 people died from the storm and the cold, including 200 in New York City alone. On top of that severe flooding occurred, in the spring, due to melting snow.

Maggie had many patients who had frost bitten their toes or fingers. One neighbor, Sam Larson, had to be out in the bad weather for quite awhile shoveling snow and clearing ice off his roof.

He went to Maggie with his fingertips turning black and feeling warm and numb. She soaked his hands for 30 minutes until his skin went back to its normal color. For his face and ears she applied a warm, wet washcloth.

With deep frostbite, the patient may experience numbness and joints or muscles may stop working. When this happened she sent these folks to the hospital. Medical treatment for them involves rewarming, medications, wound care, surgery and various therapies, depending on the severity of the frostbite.

Sam recovered from his frostbite and was able to use his hands again thanks to Maggie.

Other patients came to her with chilblains. This usually develops several hours after exposure to the cold.

Chilblains typically cause a burning and itching sensation in the hands or feet, which can become more in tense if you go into a warm room. The affected skin may also swell and turn red or dark blue.

Maggie's treatment for chilblains was to keep the hands and feet warm and dry, avoiding cold, wet environments and wearing warm, dry clothing. She had patients exercise and stay warm to improve their circulation.

During the two weeks that Maggie and her family were trapped indoors she was able to feed them from her large pantry of canned goods that she had put up in the fall. She had canned everything from vegetables and fruit to ham and bacon. She had chickens, who survived the storm in their coop, so they were able to have eggs with their breakfast.

Another story she liked to tell her grandkids was of the huge fire that burned down most of their county.

The Great Marquette County Fire was caused by the same winds that fanned the Great Chicago Fire. Some believe lightning started this fire where several cities, towns and villages, including Negaunee burned extensively.

The operation of lumber mills left behind branches, bark and quantities of unused wood which was perfect tinder for a large fire. Most areas had had no rain in months, making the dried-up vegetation and logging debris fuel for the fires.

Not only was the land burnt and left barren, thousands of buildings were destroyed with no lumber left to rebuild. Hundreds of families were left homeless. Some estimates put the loss of life at 500.

The Foleys had to live in a tent until their house was rebuilt. Maggie didn't mind. She felt lucky that none of her family or friends were killed or injured in the fire.

Since her children were grown and gone they didn't have to build such a large house. They were happy with their new, 2 bedroom bungalow.

The worst part of the fire for Maggie was the loss of her family photos. She did write to her extended family to see if any of them had extra copies she could have. Luckily she was able to get photos of her parents and her family when they were young.

Maggie was in demand for her midwife skills and for other illnesses that made their way through her small town of Negaunee.

Most women were still giving birth at home back then, as hospitals weren't widely available and were generally for sick patients. In rural America midwives at tended up to 75% of births until the 1940s.

Common options for coping with pain in childbirth were massage, water therapy, and breathing exercises.

Maggie had her ladies take short walks or change positions during labor, since moving around can reduce pain.

The typical American woman bore an average of 7 children. She had her first child around the age of 23 and proceeded to bear a child every two-years.

Maggie would also help her women find birth control if they had too many children or if her health was at stake. Back then this included spermicides, douches, an early diaphragm called the Dutch cap, and ergot pills which induced terminations.

Maggie was helpful to her neighbors when they became ill with measles, cholera, influenza, pneumonia, diarrhea, accidents, or diphtheria.

She had what she called a 'bag of tricks' that she always had on hand that held remedies, tools and instruments of her trade.

For cholera she helped to rehydrate the patient. Care for a person with measles would include resting, eating well, and drinking plenty of fluids. For influenza the treatment was the same as cholera and to get more sleep to help their immune system fight infection. Pneumonia called for getting enough rest and drinking warm fluids such as ginger or fenugreek tea. For diarrhea she ad ministered colonic irrigants and purgatives.

Diphtheria was a serious infection caused by bacteria that make a toxin in the body. It can lead to difficulty breathing, heart rhythm problems, and even death.

Maggie did her best for these patients but there wasn't much she could do if they progressed to the critical stage and this is when she would send them to the hospital.

Scrofula was another ailment she dealt with. It is swollen glands of the neck and is also called tuberculosis of the neck. Some affected individuals experience fatigue, fever, and weight loss.

There was no reliable treatment for Scrofula back then so she made these patients as comfortable as she could and the disease ran its course. She knew that some physicians prescribed bleedings and purgings, but most often, doctors simply advised their patients to rest, eat well, and exercise outdoors. Very few recovered.

In the case of accidents such as a broken arm or leg she was handy at making a splint that the patient would wear for 6 weeks. For burns she used aloe to soothe the pain. At times she used honey and tannic acid to heal burns.

In the old days they knew that honey, moldy bread and copper salts could prevent infections in burns and other skin issues while healing. Maggie always carried these with her. Mullein leaves & flowers are anti-inflammatory, antiseptic, antispasmodic, astringent & expectorant. It's one of Maggie's go-to remedies for respiratory illnesses.

One story that she didn't tell her grandkids was when she was held hostage by criminals.

Maggie was treating a woman out in the bad part of town when she was taken hostage. The woman, Shelby Talbot, was suffering with a bad case of rickets and Maggie was treating her with cod liver oil by mouth every day for 5 weeks to cure it.

Shelby was a mousy young woman who had a violent brother who lived with her. George brought home unsavory men of all types and on this day he showed up with Glen Rudeck who had a case of hives. Maggie put calamine on his rash but then he asked her to come with him to his dads home who had an unknown ailment. Maggie said she couldn't go with him because she was expected at home for supper and proceeded to leave.

Glen grabbed her by the throat and shoved her up against the wall and said, "If you don't come with me I'll kill your friend Shelby here."

Maggie squeaked out, "Don't you touch her," and went limp under his hand. She went with him to keep these men from causing any more trouble. Glen got her into the back of his wagon and they left town, driving for what seemed like hours.

They arrived at a ramshackle place where Glen's dad lived. When Maggie first saw Henry she thought, "This man looks dead," but she asked, "How long has he been like this?"

Glen responded, "He's been sick for around 10 days."

"You should have sent for me sooner. I don't know if I can help him much."

"Get to work and make him better. That's what you do for everyone else in town so do it now," said Glen.

Maggie made a show of treating him knowing she had to act the part to stay alive. She got out some herbs and made a tea that Henry drank. She also gave him some pills, just Aspirin, and told him to chew them hoping they would quickly give him some temporary relief so that she might be able to escape.

She also made a tea for Glen and George that had a strong dose of a sleeping remedy in it. Soon the two were snoozing away and Maggie slipped out of the cabin and ran.

And did she run. She ran like never before because she was running for her life. She was quickly in the woods on a path that she hoped would take her back to town.

But this wasn't the way to go. She was just running deeper into the woods where she became disoriented and lost.

Glen and George had gone after her but soon tired of searching for her so they went back to the cabin to find that Henry was dead. They wailed in grief for quite awhile then Glen said, "We have to find that bitch. She killed dad. She has to die. George agreed and they ran out and into the woods trying to follow her trail.

Maggie knew the woods like the back of her hand. This was where she sought out her herbs and plants for her work. She knew where there was a cave and made her way there to hide from the "G" boys.

The cave was at the top of a gradual slope and she could see quite a ways from there and she saw them approaching her hideaway so she crept further into the cave, curled up into a ball and not stress out.

Glen and George searched high and low for Maggie but they didn't find her so they went back to town. Maggie spent the night in the cave then made her way back to her home. On the way she stopped at the Sheriffs office to report the 2 men for assault. Maggie had known Sheriff Nordstrom for many years and hoped he would be able to arrest the 2 culprits.

Glen and George were arrested 2 days later and put in jail. Maggie testified at their trial and they both were sent to prison for a year. Maggie worried that when they got out they might come after her but she had to go about her daily duties and tried not to think about them.

Back in the 1800s patients with diabetes didn't live for long. There wasn't much Maggie could do for them but put them on a very strict diet eating less carbohydrates.

This could buy patients a few extra years but couldn't cure them.

Some doctors prescribed bloodletting or opium prescriptions and also high caloric diets for counteracting the diabetes and some prescribed the "oat-cure", "potato therapy" and the "starvation diet." None of these worked well. Maggie saw that it was fasting and not an excess of calories that improved their symptoms.

One humorous myth about diabetes was 'Ants on your urine." It states that if ants go to where your urine is, it means you have diabetes. The fact is when blood sugar is above the kidney's threshold, sugar tends to spill into the urine making it "sweet", but it doesn't mean that you have diabetes if there are ants around your urine. When a patient brought this up Maggie just laughed and said there was nothing true about that myth.

Maggie's family was always turning up with some ailment or other. When her daughter, Catherine had her first baby there was an issue with the birth. The child was stuck in the birth canal so Maggie had to use forceps to get the child out. This was painful for Catherine and it also left a mark on the baby's head. Maggie told her daughter, "Those marks will be gone in a month so don't worry about them."

A month later Maggie's son Dave turned up with a sore throat. He was worried, " I've heard that if it's strep throat it can lead to Scarlet Fever which can be deadly,"

His mother told him, "Right now it's just a sore throat so don't be jumping the gun."

She had him gargle with salt water, drink fluids and, suck on hard candys and rest. He was fine after a few days.

It wasn't long after that her daughter Mary complained of a headache that she had had for 3 days. She said, "I've had throbbing pain on the right side of her head, pain behind her eyes, a bit of nausea and a sensitivity to light."

Maggie said, "What you are having is a migraine head ache and you should drink a tea of the cañahua plant. I have some with me. I will also massage your scalp which sometimes helps. Stay in a dark room and drink plenty of water."

It was after this that her husband started complaining of a lung problem. He had a bad cough and was sure he had pneumonia. His wife told him, "What you have is chronic catarrh and we will take good care of you so it doesn't develop into pneumonia. Some doctors are calling this bronchitis."

Maggie treated him with garlic, pepper, cinnamon and turpentine. His ailment lasted 8 days then he rallied and got back to work.

Maggie was relieved when her husband was on the mend because she was tired of listening to him complain. She got enough of that on the job.

Another story Maggie liked to tell her grandkids is when the town was flooded. Torrential rains hit the Negaunee area back in 1890, coming down for 3 days, and Teal Lake jumped its banks and flooded the town.

At first it was just misting and then it changed to light rain and then it was a downpour. Folks moved their furniture and household goods to the second floor where they waited for rescue.

The town received 4.3 inches of rain from Friday, May 12 to Sunday, May 14. As floodwaters spread they threaten lives, inundated properties and destroyed be longings. The flood lead to a landslide that hit part of the town.

The impact of the flood included loss of human life, damage to property, destruction of crops, loss of live stock, and the deterioration of health conditions owing to waterborne diseases.

This flood caused power, water, and gas outages. It disrupted transportation routes, polluted drinking water, and damaged homes, buildings, and roads.

Floods are now the #1 natural disaster on the planet. 90% of natural disasters in the United States involve flooding.

The Foleys survived the flood and their house wasn't hit too badly. It had about 1 inch of water that flooded the home but this receded when the surge pulled back.

They heard that 3 people died because of the flood. The town folk were relieved there weren't more.

Maggie had her hands full cleaning up after the flood. She had to throw out her rugs and other furniture that was water logged and getting moldy. She then organized a work team of women who met at one of their homes and cleaned it then moved on to another home. It took them a couple of weeks before these places were back to normal.

To avoid problems from a future flood the folks of Negaunee

planted dense vegetation, trees and shrubs to create areas of high friction that can slow advancing storm surges and protect land development.

Maggie and James continued to work for their com munity. Maggie delivered many babies and helped folks with their minor health issues. James worked his mines and volunteered his help to the town in different roles including to provide people with a direct voice in their grassroots government.

Most of Maggie's life was spent in service to others. She took care of her family in the best way possible and she helped her friends and neighbors with their medical problems and in many other ways. She was considered one of the towns leading citizens who's opinion was often sough on any number of subjects.

Margaret had a stroke in 1900 and suffered with this paralysis for 9 months before she died on December 24, 1909. She was known to a large number of Negaunee's residents as "Grandma" Foley and beloved by all. During her long and painful illness she kept a cheerful disposition and her cheery view of life was an inspiration to all she knew. She was buried in Negaunee having lived a long life of 81 years there.

James was in a shock that lasted for many days after his wife's death. His daughter came to take care of him for a few months while he got back on his feet. He had retired a few years back so his time was spent fishing and boating and visiting friends. He was thankful for the years he had with Maggie but missed her terribly and couldn't imagine life without her.

He spent as much time with his grandkids as he could teaching them about the many things he learned in life. This made him happy. He lived to the ripe old age of 87 then he was happy to join Maggie in the afterlife.

LET'S TALK

Carol Caruso

It is difficult to answer the question, "What is the most important political issue?" They all are.

My initial thought was global warming and environmental protection. That's not exclusively an American issue, and if we don't have an inhabitable planet, everything else is just a talking point. We need to start acting now if we want our children and grandchildren to have a safe place to live. Very important, but I do not feel the precision in my answer to the question.

Gun control is a topic that I want to take priority before the next mass shooting happens. I want children and teachers to be safe. I want people to be able to go to houses of worship and Walmart without worrying about being shot. For anyone who argues that I am compromising your right to bear arms, I ask you to consider the black sheep in your family or the random people you encounter on social media. Can you honestly say that "everyone" should be allowed to own a gun? How about an assault weapon? What would be the person's reason for wanting a gun? If it is protection or hunting, and the person who wants to own a gun is willing to undergo a background check, abide by the red flag law, and receive proper training, I can reluctantly agree with you. I'd ask you, in turn, to look at why the founding fathers felt the second amendment so important. We no longer live in a society where a militia is necessary, and the evolution of firearms, as well as humanity, has drastically changed. I'd like to see a world where guns aren't necessary, but I also know that Mayberry isn't real. This is an issue I'm passionate about, but I'm still not adequately addressing the answer to the initial question.

Taking care of the poor and less fortunate hits me in the heart. I don't see immigrants as "them" and it saddens me to see families fleeing their homes because they are not safe; or facing the selfless act of love that entails ensuring their children cross a border without them. Is it really about jobs? So many of us have more than enough, I don't understand why we feel threatened; we are a land of immigrants. Human suffering is wrong, and we can't stick our head in the sand. I want the world to be a better place. Where immigration is concerned, I don't claim to have all of the answers, but I believe we can be better, and we can do better.

I could continue to spew my liberal agenda, but it does no good when it falls flat on a piece of paper. We should be discussing these issues with the people that are most important in our lives without fear it will become a raging argument. If you feel I am wrong in my beliefs, intelligently educate me. I recall watching a segment of Sunday Morning about whether we should take our shoes off when we enter the house. Mo Rocca said that we like debating this issue because it is safe and keeps us from either agreeing about everything or fighting about politics. We need to be better listeners and less hostile to "otherness" when we don't agree. Let's gently find out why we disagree.

The answer to the question, therefore, is not in any one issue, but the underlying hate and divisiveness that overshadows all the issues. Bipartisanship (as it exists now) is not conducive to healing our world. It is not a matter of proving one side right or wrong but liberating both sides until we become more united. Then our thoughts can really become actionable. Communication, understanding and compromise without party affiliation may add some gray to the issues we (and the media) tend to paint so black and white.

We need young people to care about what is happening in politics. When I was younger, I didn't care, so I know this is a big ask. It doesn't matter what opinion this young generation holds, but they need to start paying attention and talking to each other. From my vantage point, the stakes are higher.

I look back to the Reagan era and hear him say that we need to make America great again, I look at the similarities between the Nixon and Trump administrations, and I wonder if we are just in continuous cycle of repeating history.

Maybe one day my young grandchildren will read this, and they'll see that our planet is not warming; it was all a hoax. I can't wrap my head around that as a truth, but I will be glad, for their sake, to be proven wrong.

ECDYSIS OF GREEN FLOWERS

Abubakar Auwal

here— an image of motherland is tuned from the rhythm
of our greened fur; a convolvulus one, taking flight
to where we plant our names, flower the smiles of gods &
    metaphors
into anything that plant home in the garden of chrysanthemum.
in another poem; *i wafted my bones into an enigma of broken nights*
waxed on the pulpit, father buried his teeth in loopholes of an early
bee— the bee is a greened flower, wearing mother's face
like a butterfly, water-flying to name the colors of dark metaphors.
here— boys & girls with broken teeth are scarfed into the cottage of
shattered dreams, like headless flowers swallowing the colors of
    death.
i'm remembering the year mother held the face of gods on her
    palms,
rewriting her womb for the birth of another god; a green one
to facebook her heart & unify her scrunching face
in between the lullabies of green clouds— green & white fur,
    flapping
in the constitution of the ashes we daily inhale
to sing the anthem of men metamorphosed into the shrine.
father thought us to live, to heart, to sun, to day, to night
and gather the debris of our broken names, together.
to tweet the route of a green home; i cultured my breath into

    appendages
of memories, morphing between the whispers of butterflies
like the wind translating our names into ecdysis of green flowers.
i engraved my ribs to learn the language of everything green.
tonight; this poem fly to home a greened dove, vanishing between
the science of a boy learning the lunatic language of desert & men.

GEORGE AND THE DRAG ON

Andrew Hough

In times, ages past in the latter days of the Roman Empire there lived a legionnaire called George Kypriano. He was from the island of Cyprus, a gallant man who longed to become a hero. His comrades mocked him saying he would never be a champion as he had such a vivid imagination and was constantly daydreaming - about slaying dragons, or rescuing maidens or aiding damsels in distress. Better informed individuals assured him that there were no such thing as dragons or giants and since the arrival of Roman legions maidens were in short supply as well. Even legionnaires who had marched up and down the roads that criss-crossed the empire admitted that they had not seen any sign of such creatures either.

But that didn't deter George. He daydreamed all the more.

One day an opportunity came for him to find out for himself. Orders were issued to every Roman soldier available to come to the aid of the Eternal city and return to Rome which was threatened with invasion. When he arrived from the sea journey he was shocked to see the damage that had already been done to that great city.

"The vandals!" cried George as he marched along the Appian Way, surveying the countless number of statues, monuments and buildings that had been damaged in the series of attacks.

"We have the same problem where I come from!" remarked his fellow patrolman.

"Where is that?" enquired George.

"An island called Britain!" was the man's response.

He had heard of that place from the Phoenician sailors who berthed at Cyprus.

"Tell me more about your country!" he enquired further.

"There's not much to tell really!" continued the Briton. "It's not been quite the same since all those roads were built. It used to be such a quiet little back water."George paused for a moment and then asked.

"Do you have any dragons in your country?"

The patrolman looked away nervously from George's gaze and snorted

"Of course not! Whatever made you think there was?"

But George could not help thinking that this was a lie.

Many years passed while George stayed in Rome, helping to defend the city from waves of Barbarian invasions. Some attempts at the city's defence were less successful than others.

"I had almost forgotten what it was like to fight!" barked the British patrolman one evening while sharing another watch with George. "We haven't been attacked for years!" he murmured

"Is that because of the Roman occupation?" he wondered aloud.But the Briton didn't reply.

One day an urgent appeal was sent from Britain to Rome. "Help!" it read, "we are being attacked by Saxons, Jutes as well as from every Angle! Send reinforcements!"

So, they did, and George was one of them. It didn't take very long to ward off the Saxons, Jutes or the Angles but George decided to stay, and in the meantime got married. He did this so that when the Romans left, he could stay behind and avoid deportation. News had reached him from the valleys in Wales of a large lizard at large in the locality. So, he took his wife by the hand and went off in search of the Welsh dragon.

When they arrived in the principality tired, hungry and worn out from their travels and travails they discovered that the dragon lived quite close to the prince's palace. Everyday a woman had to be sacrificed to the dragon in order to assuage its wrath and satisfy its monstrous appetite. George set out for the palace intending to announce his plan to rid the country of the pest. When he reached the walls of the castle, he discovered that it was surrounded by a large group of women protesting who were encamped in the scorched fields that bordered the building.

Slowly our hero approached a group of women and politely asked them what was going on. They all eyed him with suspicion and demanded to know what he wanted. Undeterred George cleared his throat before announcing that he was there to stop the dragon. The group of women fell silent before bursting into laughter.

"What do you think we are doing here?" they all cried

"That's what I want to know!" Snapped George, who by now felt rather small, and hadn't yet quite grasped the peculiarities of the English language. But this only made them laugh louder.

"Will someone please tell me what is going on around here?" He pleaded. Just then one of the women stepped forward

"Come on!" she chirped. "Let him in, he seems fairly harmless!"

The group dispersed and George was led through the camp. All around women sat singing and laughing and arguing. The camp was extensive but pretty primitive. Children ran in and out of shabby tents scattered all about the site and played in the mud. Everyone looked in need of a good wash.

The woman stopped turned to George and explained

"Sit down here for a while. If you want a drink, you'll have to find a clean cup!"

George declined the offer but sat down on the grass beside the woman. He listened carefully as she explained that the dragon had arrived some years earlier, devouring all in its path. The Prince had refused to do anything about it so the women got together and established a protest camp. Most days the guards arrived and tried to drive them away but up until now they had failed to shift anyone.

"We even mistook you for one of them!" she remarked.

"I'm not one of those! I am an officer in the Roman army who now vows to avenge everyone, man, woman and child who had died at the jaws of that detestable creature!"

The woman smiled and added

"You will find it pretty difficult to get near the thing! It's surrounded by soldiers. Anyone who tries to get anywhere near it is turned away."

He chewed these comments over then asked

"Is there no other way of getting at it?"

"The only way we get near it is when we are invited to the palace for dinner!"

"You get invited to dinner – with the Prince?"

"No – with the dragon! Everyday one of us is chosen to be sacrificed to the beast!"

"What would happen then if I marched to the Prince's palace and declared it is my intention to stop anyone else being eaten?"

"You would be arrested or laughed at! As far as the Prince is concerned the dragon deters invaders. Sacrificing one of his natives is a small price to pay for such security!"

The next day a small squad of soldiers arrived to escort another woman to dine with the dragon. George watched helplessly as the poor victim was dragged away screaming, while the others bravely surged forward in a vain attempt to thwart the guards. If anyone tried to follow, they immediately opened fire.

"This is awful!" bleated George. "What will happen to her?"

"She will be taken to the forbidden area tied to a tree and then the dragon moves in!" she explained.

"How do you know this?" he enquired.

"One day the soldiers came and took a twin who refused to let the other one go. So, they took them both – but the dragon only ate one of them!"

"How awful! Is she still alive?"

"Yes, but she won't talk to any man!"

"Then you must talk to her!"

"What for?"

"You must find out what the soldier looks like who actually takes her to the Forbidden Area. At what point is he allowed to enter? What is the password?"

The woman gave him a quizzical look then asked.

"Why do you want to know all that?"

"I have an idea!" replied George deep in thought.

That night the woman crept up to the Forbidden Area with George. Obscured by the darkness they managed to find a spot just out of view.

At first light a small detachment of soldiers left for the camp. Within minutes a soldier, dressed in full armour and carrying a shield that covered his whole body came running down the road hauling behind him the next victim, bound and ready.

"That was quick!" remarked the startled sentinel guarding the Forbidden Area.

"There's a riot back there!" explained the soldier gripping the hysterical candidate. "They seemed to be ready for us this time, so

I grabbed the first one and ran back. The others are dealing with the crowds.

The sentry stood to attention and demanded the password.

"Don't bolt the door until I get back!" barked the soldier.

The sentry withdrew to allow them both easier access. A few minutes passed when on the horizon the rest of the patrol that had set out earlier reappeared. They marched in tight formation right up to the Forbidden Area. Their captain stood staring at the sentry.

"Well?" he said.

"Any trouble?" asked the sentry.

"No more than usual! Aren't you going to ask me for the password?"

"Why should I?"

But he never completed the sentence. Suddenly behind them came a loud cry. They all turned. In the middle of the Forbidden Area stood a Roman soldier, shield and spear in hand crying in a loud voice:

"Citizens of this fair land! Do not be afraid! My name is George and I have come to slay the dragon!"

When the guards realised what had happened, they rushed forward towards the solitary figure, who now stood defiantly in the Forbidden Area. But as they moved in the sky suddenly grew darker as if a great cloud had obscured the sunlight. Everyone stopped still and looked up. There high above them was the dragon. It swooped down and over the sentries scattering them in all directions. As it came to rest in a field thedragon turned towards the spot where the victim usually awaited her fate. But instead there stood brave George, protected by his full-length shield. The dragon roared and sent flames shooting from its terrifying jaws blasting the shield. The dragon then moved in assuming the assailant had been unable to with-stand the onslaught. But the armour remained true in spite of being scorched George leapt out from behind thesecurity of the shield, and struck the dragon in the eye with his long spear. The dragon winced then retreated. Quickly George nipped out from behind his shield and took refuge behind a tree. Just in time – for on this occasion the shield was consumed in a ball of fire. As the huge lizard approached the smouldering remains George darted out from the shelter of the tree intending to attack the dragon from the rear. But he had forgotten its long tail and as it swished to and fro it knocked him to the ground. The dragon turned its ugly head towards him but George dealt a savage blow to its tail. It stepped back to cry out in pain. Once it had recovered it took a deep breath and incinerated the tree. George jumped out to escape the heat and had to dive for cover behind a nearby boulder. There he lay motionless for a few seconds. Taking hold of a rock he waited until the dragon was near enough and sent it hurling through the air. It struck the dragon full in the face. George ran for the flaming tree avoiding the dragon's furious bursts of fire. Then in a last desperate attempt he ran from the cover of the tree to where his spear lay. The dragon meanwhile half blinded from the previous attack nursed its wounded tail. Spear in hand he picked up another rock and edged his way back towards his adversary taking great care to stay out of the dragon's range of fire. He took careful aim with the rock and hit the dragon squarely on the nose. The dazed dragon let out an agonising cry skyward, exposing the soft underbelly of below its chin. Grasping his spear in his hand George drew back and hurled the spear at the dragon with all his remaining strength. But it never reached its mark. George was too exhausted, and the weapon glanced off the creature's scaly sides. Now he was helpless. Too tired to run he sank to his knees.

The dragon moved slowly towards him and poised itself for the final blow. Our hero fainted. He lay there for a few seconds and through his blurred vision saw that the dragon was now upon him. But rather than attack him the dragon seemed to be struggling with an unseen force. George opened his weary eyes wider. The creature was now contorted and twisted, crying out in desperation. From behind the dragon's hide soldiers appeared with strong ropes held in their hands. Groups of them had the monster tied and were pulling it to the ground. Recovering quickly from his daze George rushed to reclaim his spear and as it wrestled with the mass of cords that now encompassed its huge frame George struck a fatal blow to the dragon's soft underbelly. The dragon went rigid, then breathing its last spouted great flames from its jaws, keeled over and laid motionless on the ground.

For a few seconds nobody moved. They all stared at George. From behind the dead carcass stepped the captain of the guard. He marched right up to George and struck him across the face.

"What the hell were you playing at? My men had it under control and you – you had to kill it, you idiot!"

The bewildered hero was put under arrest and led away to the dungeons.

However, news of his feat spread all over the land. It was carried by the women whom George had befriended in the camp and who had all escaped in the confusion.

George's fame was an embarrassment to the whole Government not least because it was the Prince who had brought the dragon to those shores in the first place with the intention of protecting his people. The Prince believed that having something so terrifying and could inflict injury on such a vast scale would be a deterrent to any potential invader to his tiny principality. It wasn't the only country to wield such a weapon of mass destruction. Cornwall had its giants, Russia its Baba Yaga, Greece its Sphinx and even in the Highlands there were rumours of a huge monster. When the prince realised the extent of George's fame, he decided to make him a national hero. A story was told that the Prince had invited George to save them from the dragon's tyranny but when he succeeded, he left for Europe where he was martyred for his faith. But all the time the prince was determined to find another dragon. For even if it did mean the death of one female per day, wasn't peace and security worth such a sacrifice?

FOLIE À DEUX

Andi Stout

Two fragile silhouettes
in cakewalk dance
linked
by their arms, they promenade
looking in opposite directions.
He's focused on abundance.
Phthalo Evergreens stand
lush and fertile
beneath his breast,
but the valleys need water.
So, he borrows
all she has,
siphoning cobalt
from her hair, down
through their shared elbow,
and into his veins.
Her landscape
gradually becomes barren,
heart kicked out of her chest,
by two-step,
two-step,
high-knee,
a small red stain—faint,

and fading
off beside her shoulder.

This slow cycle of depletion
will persist
as long as she lets it.

TRAPPED IN TREPIDATION

Ndaba Sibanda

Our strong scales are some souls' traditional prescription,
yet we aren't that solid, they just constitute our fortification.

Sometimes souls take us as reptiles, but we're scaly animals.
Our meat and scales in great demand, we're those mammals.

We're caught and sold for dietary, medicinal or spiritual reasons.
We're an 80 million year-old species that faces a purge from
legions!

If it's not about us being their daily delicacy, it's about footwear,
as in boots, or leather products as in bags, and belts they wear.

They hunt us and turn our skins into lucrative leather goods,
our startled scales into arthritis, asthma and rheumatism cures.

We don't want to be wiped out, still, every short second,
extinction,
hounds us, we, the pained, traded pangolins trapped in
trepidation.

THEY DIDN'T CARE

Melanie Flores

They stomped on the black man
as if he was an invading cockroach -
unnecessary and reviled.
They didn't care that he was a father,
brother, son, and friend.

They left the old woman in her own feces
as if she didn't matter -
unwanted and defiled.
They didn't care that she was a mother,
grandmother, wife, and sister.

They cornered the distraught woman
as if she was a criminal –
armed and wild.
They didn't care that she wept inside
and needed compassion.

They didn't care that these people
meant something to someone,
that they laughed and cried

and had goals, hopes, and dreams,
just like you and me and everyone.

THE WORLD IS UPSIDE DOWN //
IL MONDO ALLA ROVESCIA

Barbara Anna Gaiardoni

The opposition in jail
Children are dying of hunger
Soldiers as cannon fodder
We need to be healed
There is a need of us.

L'opposizione nelle prigioni
I bambini muoiono di fame
Soldati come carne da macello
Abbiamo bisogno di essere guariti
C'è bisogno di noi.

WHEN INDOCTRINATION IS A-OK

Cecil Morris

When we demand a daily promise of school children
an exercise in allegiance, a submission each day
to symbol of state and God, a recognition
of the hierarchy we espouse and impose.
When we ask them to swear fealty to the republic
each day with acknowledgment of their subjugation,
of their underness, of the supremacy of God.
When we clothe ourselves in our flag and demand
the people salute our shirt, our cap, the words we say
while so dressed as if we speak the true red white and blue.
When we translate rights to entitlements undeserved
and alienable and subject to whims of the rich
When we wave our banners and march and chant and repeat
our lies until they resound with sound of truth and stir
our followers to rise up in credulocity unbound
by weight of reality, to rise in animus
aggrieved and angry until we pacify them
with fictitious guarantees of liberty and justice
and happiness indivisible pulled from the past
and borne to the future on the sea of their arms.

BARE BONES

Lynn White

The skeleton lies desolate
some bits and pieces
of its living
still discernible
in the bare
hot red desert.

But each day it decays
wind and rain weather it
destroying its form
and substance
until it wastes away
and fades into the landscape.

If it had come to rest further south or north
it may have sunk into boggy peat moss
and risen with hair and hide intact with,
the cause of death discernible with
its last meal of grass or rabbit
still there inside its stomach
its regularity
preserved
by nature.

Preserved or wasted.
It all depends on
where you
fall.

REFLECTION: CAN A FLAME FREEZE?

Emmanuel Umeji

Strayed in a quest for an anodyne,
A blast is folding a country in its tongue.
Another are mouths wet with devotions
Hoping a country doesn't dissolve its denizens
In its heat. Days starts with a knife
Shredding the constitution. & night
Interrupts with a mouth full of gunshots.
& a country is misrepresented to Jupiter,
Unfit to call a sanctuary. A casualty is a voice dimming
As if the bullet stoned into its body is a distance
Swallowing him up. This is how a country
Learns to drown in the blood it shed.
I am a memory chip holding all the dark lyrics
This country had ever taught a bone.
I approach home with a voice coated with ice
Hoping I'm what freezes the flame.

BLOOD ON THE FLAG

Prayerlife Onyinyechi Nwosu

Gun shots sound like a clapping thunder
The sky flames and rains blood
Bullets fly like a humming bird
As blood flows like water falls

The peaceful protest has become bloody
No to brutality; a cause for death
No to bad governance; a cause for war
Where went the democratic nation?
Leaders are calm with fewer worries

Laws of irrelevancies are imposed
Cries of poor masses ignored
Fire opened on peaceful protesters
Leaders of tomorrow killed with no sentiment
Freedom of speech is a death phrase

For how long shall we leave with fear?
Over leaders who were chosen to serve?
They have sent thugs to kill and destroy
Human right raped in the broad day
You even shoot at citizens bearing the flag

Our life jackets are now on extinct
Our flag is stained with blood of our youth
Parents have been left childless
I weep over the bloody state of my country
Reformation we ask, let love lead.

THEFT

Joseph Levens

I told him I considered myself an ingénue, nondescript, nothing other than an average woman in the city. He said there was something disturbingly sensual in my plainness. "Disturbingly sensual?" I said. "Are you sure about that?"

"I've always wanted to dine with a hero. At least for one day." He wiped his lips with the linen napkin. "Heroine, in this case. Heroine Helena."

Let me back up and explain what is going on. Six months ago, I decided to donate a kidney. There are programs for such a thing. To save another's life is almost the same as saving your own. Yet, the stipulations: I would not be told the name of the person to whom my organ was given, though I was allowed to learn the gender and age. A forty-seven-year-old male, the form read. Someone twenty years my senior. The transplant was a success. "How did you find me?" I said, after we sat down to dinner. He insisted he'd pay.

"You could learn so much by simply querying the Internet," he said, and it scared me. I gripped my wine glass.

I sometimes think of myself as a forgotten item at a tag sale, set in a corner one barely notices -- out-of-date, but homely and with its own nostalgic charm. Yes, I wanted to know who it was that received a part of me, whose life I saved. I agreed to meet him simply out of curiosity. You might think I was hoping for some sort of compensation. Perhaps the man was rich. But to make it very clear, my friend, no, that is not at all why I did what I did. Why I allowed a surgeon to open me up and take something, assuring me I would suffer no ill effects while saving another's life. Why, when contacted months afterward by the recipient and asked to dinner, I said yes.

* * *

I keep reminding myself that this is my life, not a dress rehearsal for another. We will, none of us, ever be as young again. Help the world while you can and the world will help you. So I thought.

I live in a studio apartment on the Upper East Side and teach first grade at a charter school in the Bronx. Sometimes I feel as though these kids are my life, that guiding them through the basics of living is something I am doing to make a better world.

Several years ago, my attempt to join the Peace Corps failed epically. I passed several interviews and was officially "invited" to apply. All foreseeable paths led to heaven, and I was given my assignment in Guinea, West Africa, inoculated with the vaccines, including the one for yellow fever which made me incredibly sick for a week. A month before deployment, the Peace Corps changed its mind and rejected me. Though I had given full disclosure of the one isolated night in my college dorm when I emptied the bottle of Wellbutrin, passed out, and landed in the emergency room, this was enough to cause a last-minute reversal in decision.

* * *

When the weather is nice, I step from the lighted entrance to my building and slip into the welcoming shadows of the alleyway. The night absorbs me. There, under impartial stars, in a perfect wedge of darkness, I disappear. They say the planets and constellations, even on a clear night, are hard to decipher in a big city. Not so. I have communicated with Io, the innermost moon of Jupiter. She sometimes asks me how I'm feeling, and other questions I don't quite know how to answer, but I appreciate them anyway.

* * *

And so here we were, sitting over chicken l'orange and twenty-year-old Bordeaux -- this man whose life I saved with thinning hair swept across the top of his head, as though trying to hide a growing baldness. He gripped his water glass with fingertips set just so, and it started to make me uneasy. I was hoping he would be a bit more reserved, but you already know that. "You are a saint," he said. "My savior. My superhero. My salvation."

And my impatience grew. Here was not sincerity. Here was not genuine and humble gratitude. The sensuality of my plainness occupied the very forefront of tonight's dinner, dominated it, hung in the heavy air over the table candles. It drove the man so.

"Think of us now," he said. "Both you and I operationally sound, sprung from your very self." He held his hands in the air. "As if you'd given me rebirth." He moved his arms higher. "As if we are not two, but one." I looked away as he slowly brought his fingers together, entwining them over his head.

I wondered if he'd next show me the scar, beneath which would be something borne from *my* very body, not his. I felt myself getting sick.

And so ended the night.

* * *

This morning, I did some reading on famous artwork and calamity. Just because I felt like it. I learned that shortly after midnight, on March 18th, 1990, at the Isabella Stewart Gardner Museum in Boston, two men dressed as police officers entered the building. When a relief guard reported for duty the next morning, he noticed several of his comrades handcuffed to pipes in the basement, and as the day wore on it was discovered that thirteen classic paintings were no longer hanging on the walls of the museum.

Among the works stolen in the largest property crime in United States history was Johannes Vermeer's "The Concert." This oil on canvas was painted by the artist circa 1665. Partly due to Vermeer's uniquely limited body of work – a total of some thirty paintings – "The Concert," should it ever reemerge, is estimated to fetch approximately a quarter of a billion dollars, making it the most valuable painting whose whereabouts is unknown.

Today, in the exact spot "The Concert" hung, visitors see an empty frame. Today, should you peek inside me, you will see something missing as well.

* * *

Later in the day, on the phone, I spoke to my mother. A retired school teacher on Long Island, she now leads Monday night home extension classes in the local school district. I told her that to-morrow is Inside-Out Pajama Day at school.

"They never had that when I taught," she said. "It's silly but sounds like fun. You have to wear pajamas as well as the kids?"

"Yes. Inside-out."

She asked about the dinner, the man with the newfound kidney.

"It was like the perfect crime," I said, and gave the sordid details.

"They should screen people better," she said. "Maybe they could have had you meet the person and let you to decide if he or she was worthy."

"Worthy?"

"Yes."

I thought for a moment. I was not sure *worthy* was a suitable word.

"Without people like me," I said, "the man would have died."

"And the world would have been better off, Helena."

My mother has never been a cruel person, and this comment surprised me a bit. She goes to Mass every Sunday and apologizes for things beyond her control, like an afternoon filled with rain or the price of strawberries at the market in winter. But I understood why she said what she did. It sprung from the classic love of a mother for her daughter.

"What's important," I said, "is to do the right thing."

"Allow me a moment while I fetch my violin, please," she said. I could picture her eyes momentarily cast toward the ceiling.

"I saved a life, Mom." I paused. "He now has a second chance, this Derek or Dirk, I think his name was. Or maybe Dick."

"Dick," my mother said. "Yes, I'm sure that was his name."

* * *

I order dinner sometimes from a deli called Happy, one block away. A small Mexican man brings me a garden salad-for-one, fresh fruit, Eggplant Rollatini. I insist there be no plastic; every small thing matters in this life. The intercom rings and when I ask who is there I hear my favorite word: "Happy." After buzzing him in and opening my door, there my little man stands, holding out the white bag.

A neighbor, a nice older woman whose name is MariEllen, recently told me that for many years an old, quiet man lived in my apartment. A World War II medic. No wife. Then he died. I am the succeeding tenant, MariEllen said. I live here with him, now -- his ghost. He is not a mean person. He hovers in the air, listens to my phone conversations, sits across the kitchen table when I eat. He watches me sleep too, from the rocking chair by the window. They say ghosts are evil, but my war medic ghost is not. He is my guardian. Everyone needs one. I feel safe knowing he has served time protecting our country and now watches over me in a life he is living that may have been reserved for him and those blown to pieces in an ambush.

* * *

What are the words for how we stand here in the midst of things? I am a woman of modest means. Most of what I know I have learned to first imagine. I do not shop on Fifth Avenue. I am not filled with regret and bitterness because of it.

I may, at times, feel as though I am in the ending of a movie when the camera zooms out and the stricken protagonist becomes indistinguishable from everything else down the cobblestone street, but when I think long about this, concentrate and focus and hone in, I find that these thoughts are very much unsubstantiated. You can feel diminished as you grow older and begin to realize how big the world really is, but I feel it is up to you to realistically set the frame of the image within which you live.

* * *

Last week in school, little Justin overheard a fellow teacher wish me a happy birthday, and the next morning, before even taking off his coat, he handed me a little envelope. He asked me to open it. I did.

"It's a gift card," Justin said, looking directly into my eyes. Then he pointed to it. "You can buy anything you want with that."

I wanted to kiss him on the forehead. Not everything about the world is theft and loss, driving you to exercise utmost care when turning each corner.

* * *

On my dresser is a paper survey the hospital gave me to fill out after my recovery at home was complete. A return envelope was attached, postage paid. How nice. Some of the questions:

- Overall, how would you rate your entire hospital visit?

- If there is something our staff could have done better, please describe in full.

- How do you feel about the valuable donation you provided?

- Would you recommend this experience to others?

* * *

One of my best friends in college also tried enlisting in the Peace Corps after graduation. Frieda, like me, was rejected, but for different reasons. Let's just say they were related to observing – or *not* observing – the law. She now works at a nonprofit for marine life preservation, and idles much of her time turtle-watching on beaches in the tropics, helping hatchlings. Months ago, I asked her how she liked her job.

"It's boring," she said. "And I rarely see any newborns make a run for it, come out from the hole in the dunes and safely reach the ocean. That's why I am there – because predatory birds could snatch them away, or they could start their journey in the wrong direction and die without water. I've rarely had the occasion, and most days nothing happens at all, but that's not important. What's important is that you are working your part, that you are making a difference." This helped convince me to do what I did.

* * *

My mother called again this evening.

"I'm sorry, Helena," she said. "I may have been too harsh on the man, earlier." She paused. "I can't believe I said that word. I apologize to all the many good Richards and Dicks out there in the world, and wish no evil upon anyone." After a pause, "Maybe he just acted strangely because he didn't know how to contain his gratitude."

"No, Ma," I said. "A woman knows."

"I think not, dear. You may be just stepping across the no-returns, no-refunds line of adulthood once again."

"Shall I remind you I am twenty-seven?"

"And I am fifty-four, and still learning how to sort some things. It's scary." "What is scary," I said, "is you defending Dear Dick's disposition. Why the sudden change?"

She sighed. "So how are you feeling, anyway?"

"I am fine." I looked over to my dresser. "The hospital wants me to complete a survey giving my comments on the whole ordeal."

"What are you going to write?"

"I'm not," I said.

"Honey, you need to share your thoughts, so they can make the system better."

"The system sucks, Mom." I paused. "I try to help a community in need in Africa… they don't allow it, despite how helpful I might have been. I try to save a deserving life with a part pulled from my body, risking my own fucking health, and wind up saving a dirt bag. Nothing's changed. Do you remember when I had that salt water tank with that colorful scorpionfish, and I gave it lettuce one day? I took its life when I was only trying to feed it."

"You *can't* look at things that way, Helena."

I paused.

"I know," I said.

* * *

Last week, after receiving my birthday gift at school, Melissa, who sits directly behind Justin in the classroom, turned to him and asked why he gave me what he did. It didn't surprise me, the next day, when she walked up to the front of the room and placed a drawing in crayon on my desk – a woman with my hair color standing next to a little girl holding a cake with many candles set upon it, burning bright.

For several days afterward, as other students in my class learned I breached my next year, they too sent best wishes in a variety of ways, each of which, when whittled to its very core, told me to keep at it, continue doing what I do, stay the course.

THERE'S SOMETHING

Irina Tall Novikova

There's something underneath the surface

as a designation of her words

And her thoughts

Possible

The one who dies at dawn

When the world wakes up...

But water, it's like ghosts

She herself is full of foam and dark Pisces,

Which seem like thoughts...

And everyone pesters her

Trying to take you deeper...

But it goes out like an unbloomed lamp

Which has no oil

For the scorching fire...

MY PIPE BOMB DREAM

Dotty LeMieux

In my pipe bomb dream, the pipes are filled
with sweet smelling flowers—
roses and jasmine, honeysuckle and lavender.

They soothe when opened, with alyssum and calendula.
They bind up wounds and take away cares,
unfurrow brows and unknot joints.

They avert all wars,
explode with a pop of bubbles
filled with fairy dust and fantasy.

My pipe bomb dream is powder soft,
puppy warm, new mown hay
promising.

Now wouldn't that be the America you'd like to live in?
Where unexpected packages of joy explode in your face?
Where hands are raised in welcome not forbidding?
Where pixies and unicorns and, of course,
peace love and always harmony?

I have not turned out to be
the sort of person my mother was hoping for

or the opening lines of the poem
might have led you to believe.
And I know it will not cheer you to think
that my pipe bomb dream may turn out to be
your worst nightmare.

But that's the landscape you have grown
tended and cultivated, filled with landmines
not nourishment, sudden flash and pain
not joy.

A poem without an end

VERILY

Patricia Thrushart

Amen to her bent head
with no veil.
Amen to her hair.
Amen to their raised fists,
to his bent knee.
Amen to the corner prophet
cursing war. Amen to his placard.
Amen to the handmaid
on the courthouse steps.
Amen to her red robe.
Amen to the hungry monk,
to his empty bowl.
Amen to the mother who demands
the body of her son. Amen to the son.
Amen to the man chained to a crane.
Amen to the standing rock.
Amen to the crowd linking arms at the bridge.
Amen to the bridge.
Amen to the student facing a gun.
Amen to his flower.
Amen to the artist who paints on concrete,
to his aerosol can.
Amen to the pink hats,

the gold and blue flags,
the rainbows,
the umbrellas,
the cries for peace,
the blank sheets of paper,
the poet, fallen silent.
Amen to his daughter.
Amen to the black-winged kite wheeling
over the smoldering fields.
Amen to the fields.

THIS AARDVARK

Peter F. Crowley

I've been living next to this aardvark over here and it's really brutal.

This aardvark thinks that because she doesn't make a good wage and there are big companies dominating life, that government should be flushed down the toilet, pointing to Pol Pot, Mao and Stalin.

The aardvark wonders aloud where all the termites have gone. It's the woods, I tell her, they're not what they used to be – there are hardly any trees left. Then she says, "Make America Great Again" and I wonder if she wants to go back pre-1965 when aardvarks from darker skinned countries were barred from entering. The neighborhood is not the same, she mumbles. I wonder aloud whether because now that she has Haitian, Brazilian and Chinese neighbors – are they so different from the neighbors she had when growing up. "Our neighbors eat ants," she explains. Oh, the horror. She grumbles and goes back into her burrow.

Sometimes she comes out in the pouring rain and screams at the top of her lungs. I ask what the matter is, and she says she's just blowing off steam. She was watching a *Fox News* segment about the "migrant invasion" at the border. Nearly everyone is turned away at the gates, I say, so what else to do besides cross the Rio Grande or trudge through the desert and often end up dead. The countries they left have largely been defecated on by us or dominated in ways that life has become unbearable. It kind of makes an aardvark need refuge, you know? "I have no sympathy. They bring in fentanyl and cause our children to OD." I reply that's just another tale to fuel hatred towards aardvarks who are from someplace else and don't look like you.

One day I saw her chewing on an ant. I thought you didn't like ants, I say. She nods and says she doesn't but whatever, right, she has to eat something. Plus, they aren't so bad. But the Haitians, Chinese and Brazilians eat them, I remind her. So, what, she says. That's not their main problem. The Chinese hang their laundry in weird ways, Haitians use really strange toothbrushes and Brazilians only come out at night. Aren't we all nocturnal? I ask. She ignores me and looks around for more ants to eat.

I say how horrible it was that another black aardvark was killed by police. You'd think that the cops would stop by now, even for their own self-interest, with the national spotlight on them.

She shakes her head and says, "Never say that about our heroes. It's all lies. The ones who were killed are criminals and got exactly what they deserved."

Snowflakes fall.

"You cannibal," I say, watching as she leaps off the ground and tries to gobble them up.

EXTOLLING THE OTHER HALF

Mohammed Haseen Ahmed

Women are the true embodiment of men and vice versa
Women are the true adornment of all that the universe
    encompasses
Without them the earth is left untethered, untended and scorched
Let the womb of all creations divine multiply of its kind
To flourish fervently without any fretful fright
Forgive those who forgive thy not
You are the epitome of mercy and charity, mother Mary and Teresa,
Men's atonement lies under your feet and all their remarkable feats
    are nothing but signs of defeat without you!
Mankind has always been unkind to you
Mocking, menacing, minatory muzzling your inner clamour for
    Justice divine
But despair not they will perish in repentance abound
Realising the rarity of the other kind as the harbinger of all
    bounties of self-sacrifices, motherhood, untold sufferings of the
        pangs of birth and upbringing,
Crying in silence, shedding no tears to be seen
Gruntled in groaning, never bemoaning their fates,
God has promised them paradise hereafter as they would be
    transcended into the realms of Xanadu!
Oh! Women, though you are resigned in predicament, left decrepit
    in a lurch by the same

Who conceived you, bore you, nurtured you, nourished you from
the naissance,
Shameful? Sordid saga of sanguine ingratitude towards those who
brought you into being:
Men, it is time for the much-awaited rapprochement, raise up
your daughters to relive your unfulfilled dreams, ambitions and
wishful desires,
Only they will open the gates of the gardens

VOICELESS

Rob Rolfe

(Part of *Gaza Poems*)

Gaza / Palestine

unable to breathe
or take shelter

silenced by leaders
who detest us

shunned in a land
without justice

in this war peace
is a dirty word

EVERY WORD AN ELEGY

Joie Ocampo

From the River to the Sea

Whenever Iya speaks, it's with a voice that's not her own.

It's hard to speak when she feels the vibrations in her larynx and the shapes her mouth makes but hears something else escape. Every whisper comes out a scream, every cry of sorrow becomes one of rage.

As far as she understands it, the voice she speaks with is the voice of her people. The clamor of a race reduced to spirits and graves. Hers is a cacophony of noises blending together into a semblance of speech clawing out of her throat. It's painful, and more than once she chokes on bile and spit and unsaid grievances. By the end of it, her eyes and mouth and tongue burn with the feeling of her people's dying words getting stuck between her teeth.

So Iya speaks with a voice not her own. Not entirely. Not in the way her friends use their lips to spread gossip about who they like, and who's dating who. Not in the way her peers carry complaints on their tongue about the homework due the next day. Not in the way her brother babbles without needing things to make sense. She wishes she could, but she couldn't.

All Iya can speak about is the dying moments of her people, and the hardest thing about it is that no one seems to want to listen.

No one cares that a girl of her age and stature speaks of gunfire of a century-old conflict. When heads turn as she voices out a rage that is older than she will ever be, it is to admonish her. Who is she to know about what she's talking about? Who is she to think her words are law?

Foolish girl, who would ever want to listen to her when she can barely understand herself? Foolish girl, who would ever want to understand the things she says? When each bombshell feels literal in her mouth, and her ears ring with the whistle of missiles whenever she talks?

She asks her mother why. She asks her mother how anyone could live with the burden of keeping an entire nation's history alive. Why must she be the voice of 25,000 corpses? Why must they be corpses, dying as refugees in a soil that was rightfully theirs?

Her mother tells her it is duty that compels her to speak. A duty to her people, and not to corpses or to bombs. A duty to her homeland that remains still even under rubble. Each time she opens her mouth, her mother says, is an act of defiance. A refusal to remain silent.

"My dear," her mother says, "you may become anything you want to be, but you may not be silent. You can never be silent. It is not in your blood and your name to be silent."

Her blood, her name. Rawiya. Storyteller. Not writer, not artist. Storyteller. And the stories she speaks of are on the verge of extinction. Stories of a river and a sea and all the graves paving the roads in between. Stories of watermelons and juices flowing like canals of blood where people once stood. Stories of homes leveled by weapons, and homes forcefully deserted.

Sometimes, though, she tells the story of those choosing to stay. Of those choosing to fight. Of those who look at the guns and tanks and missiles and through her lips dare to say, *"we are still here, and we will remain here. We will remain until we are free, and this soil can become sacred with olive trees and not with corpses. We will stay like we always have stayed. From the river to the sea, we will be free."*

So she continues to tell stories, even when her throat gets clogged up with the pleas of 10,000 children buried under debris and it hurts to breathe. When she gossips with her friends, she tells them stories of the man who kept taking photos even when all there was around him was destruction. While her classmates complain about homework, she complains of the artists who lost limb and livelihood, but never their voracity for life. When her brother babbles, she answers back about all the families torn apart, and those who remain to tell their tales. When she speaks, she speaks about the people who will one day be free.

Iya speaks with a voice not her own. Not exactly. Not entirely. Though she speaks with the might of a people aching to be acknowledged, with pleas for a ceasefire and recognition and freedom, sometimes she hears her own voice alongside theirs. Their cries are her cries. The cries of her people. An elegy, but a protest all the same.

SOCIAL JUSTICE AGAINST
GENDER DISPARITY

Baby Satpathy

On March 8th, 2017, the Unzip Open Mic event, held on International Women's Day at Bhubaneswar, Odisha, provided a much-needed platform for women to share their stories of facing gender bias, abuse, and the suppression of their ambitions. As women after women courageously took the stage, sharing their painful experiences via stand-ups, jokes, and poems to make them palatable, it reminded us once again that the challenges and injustices women face are not isolated incidents but rather the result of deep-rooted societal norms and patriarchal structures that systematically disadvantage women.

Some women spoke of being passed over for promotions at work in favor of male colleagues, despite being equally or more qualified. Others shared harrowing experiences of sexual abuse at the hands of trusted family members, exposing how even the home is often not a safe haven for girls. Many women poured out their anguish at being forced to put their own dreams and ambitions on the back burner to cater to their husband's needs and expectations. Time and again, the same theme emerged - women being treated as second-class citizens, their autonomy and potential stifled by the patriarchal belief that men's desires and goals take precedence.

Tanaya Patnaik, the organizer of Unzip Open Mic, saw the event as a vital platform for all these diverse experiences - a space where both the squeezed and the strong, the rebels and the restrained, could come together and speak their truth. She recognized that sexual abuse and harassment are not just common experiences for women but terrifyingly rampant - a reality that is too often shrouded in silence and shame.

For many of the speakers, stepping on stage at Unzip Open Mic represented more than just breaking their silence - it was a powerful act of reclamation. The event celebrated every facet of these women's journeys - their flaws and missteps as much as their successes and moments of joy. Ultimately, Unzip Open Mic was a celebration of womanhood in all its complexity and diversity. It underscored the importance of women claiming their right to speak out - not just in moments of crisis but whenever they feel moved to do so.

Throughout the Unzip Open Mic event, a common thread emerged in the speakers' stories - a sense of awe and appreciation for the incredible resilience and strength of women. Many described feeling privileged to belong to such a fierce, creative, and emotionally powerful community. The speakers emphasized the importance of women discussing the challenges they've faced openly and honestly, without shame or self-censorship. By coming together to share and discuss these experiences, women can remind each other of their inherent power and beauty, even in the face of a society that often devalues them.

The atmosphere at the event was one of joyful celebration and solidarity, with the audience cheering and applauding each speaker. One of the speakers at the event was the author of this article herself, who chose to express herself in her native Odia language. Through humorous anecdotes and heartfelt poetry, she encapsulated the paradoxical experience of being a woman - the way one can feel burdened and blessed by womanhood in equal measure.

Women face a multitude of challenges and barriers from the moment they enter this world, simply by virtue of their gender. The deep-rooted patriarchal norms that govern our society place them in a position of vulnerability and subordination from the very beginning. As girls grow up, they become increasingly aware of the gender-based disparities that shape their lives. The expectation is that they will eventually marry and dedicate themselves to serving their husband and in-laws, often at the cost of their own dreams and ambitions.

It is this lack of a stable identity and support structure that leaves women particularly vulnerable to abuse and exploitation. We can broadly categorize people's responses to this issue into five types:

i. The abusers themselves, who have a vested interest in maintaining the status quo.

ii. Those who have never personally experienced or witnessed domestic violence and therefore struggle to understand the gravity of the problem.

iii. Victims who have internalized their abuse to such an extent that they are unable to recognize it as such and may even blame themselves.

iv. Those who are aware that they are being abused but feel powerless to speak out or seek help.

v. The brave survivors who dare to break the silence and speak their truth.

We must all work to challenge the deep-seated attitudes and structures that enable gender-based violence and discrimination to persist. This means questioning the societal norms that devalue women, supporting survivors, and holding abusers accountable.

Many people assume that abuse always involves physical violence, but emotional abuse can be just as damaging, leaving invisible scars that may take years to heal. Abusers are often master manipulators, skilled at making their victims feel dependent and powerless. As the abuser's control escalates, they often employ tactics of isolation, cutting their victim off from family and friends who might offer support or challenge their behavior.

It's important to recognize that abuse is never the victim's fault, no matter what the abuser may claim. However, the psychological manipulation and trauma of abuse can make it extraordinarily difficult for victims to break free, even when they intellectually recognize that what they are experiencing is wrong.

A person's inability to leave an abusive relationship is often rooted in their childhood experiences and conditioning. Women who choose to stay with violent partners may have had their defense mechanisms systematically broken down over years of trauma and manipulation, often starting in their formative years. It's crucial to recognize that this dynamic can affect women from all walks of life, regardless of their intelligence, education level, or professional success.

Ultimately, healing from abuse is not just an individual journey but a collective responsibility. We must create a culture that believes and supports survivors, providing them with the resources and validation they need to reclaim their lives.

Sati, the horrific practice of a widow immolating herself on her husband's funeral pyre, was a deeply entrenched custom in ancient India. It took the tireless efforts of courageous social reformers like Iswar Chandra Vidyasagar and Raja Ram Mohan Roy to abolish this barbaric tradition and pave the way for the freedoms that women enjoy today. However, as we reflect on this dark chapter in history, we must ask ourselves: what were the roots of this devastating practice? What beliefs and power structures enabled it to persist for so long, in the face of such immense human suffering?

The idea that women are inherently incapable or inferior is not born out of ignorance but rather out of a deliberate effort to maintain gender-based power imbalances. The story of flight Lieutenant Shivangi Singh, the first woman to fly a Rafale fighter jet in the Indian Air Force, is a powerful testament to what women can achieve when they are given the chance to soar. Her historic achievement shatters the notion that women are unfit for combat roles or leadership positions in the military.

Similarly, when husbands and in-laws confine women to the domestic sphere, demanding that they focus solely on household chores and childcare, they are actively working to limit women's horizons and prevent them from developing the skills and knowledge that could challenge male dominance. The fact remains that the subjugation of women is not an accident or a misunderstanding - it is a deliberate and systemic effort to maintain patriarchal control. Overcoming this oppression requires a sustained and collective effort to dismantle the legal, economic, and cultural barriers that keep women confined and constrained.

The story of Rani Lakshmibai, the legendary Queen of Jhansi, is a powerful testament to the resilience and indomitable spirit of women in the face of oppressive gender norms. Born into a progressive family, Lakshmibai (affectionately known as Manu) was raised in a manner typically reserved for sons, learning to ride elephants and horses and to wield weapons with skill and confidence. However, Lakshmibai's life took a drastic turn upon her marriage to the King of Jhansi. Suddenly, she found herself confined to the palace, her movements and activities severely restricted by the expectations of her new role.

But Lakshmibai refused to be cowed by these limitations. With remarkable ingenuity and determination, she assembled a regiment of female soldiers from among her maidservants, training them in the art of warfare. Following the death of her husband, Lakshmibai further subverted traditional gender roles by resuming her military training and expanding her all-female army. Her exceptional bravery and strategic acumen in defending Jhansi against British forces earned her a place in history as one of India's most celebrated freedom fighters.

Lakshmibai's story finds echoes in the life of another trailblazing Indian woman: Indira Gandhi, the first and only female Prime Minister of India to date. Despite her immense political accomplishments, Gandhi's journey was marred by the constant need to prove herself in a male-dominated world. The fact that Gandhi felt compelled to sign her letters to her father, Jawaharlal Nehru, as "from your loving Indu boy" speaks volumes about the pressure she faced to conform to masculine ideals of strength and leadership.

As we reflect on these stories, it is crucial to recognize that the goal is not to demonize individual men or husbands but rather to challenge the broader systems of patriarchy that enable and perpetuate gender-based oppression. We must work to create a world in which women's dignity, autonomy, and right to self-determination are non-negotiable - a world in which no woman is ever forced to choose between her personal aspirations and the expectations of her marital or familial roles.

From the moment they reach adolescence, many individuals who menstruate are forced to endure an excruciating ordeal every month, one that is often dismissed as a natural and inevitable part of being female. The pain that accompanies menstruation, particularly during the first day of bleeding, can be nothing short of debilitating for many. And yet, despite the immense suffering it causes, this pain is rarely taken seriously as a legitimate health concern. Instead, girls and women are expected to simply bear this burden in silence, their agony hidden away behind closed doors and stoic faces.

The point I want to drive home is that an alarming number of women in our lives - our daughters, wives, sisters, and daughters-in-law, are suffering immensely during their menstrual cycles. The pain they endure, particularly from the debilitating cramps, can be as severe as the agony of childbirth. Yet, instead of being met with understanding and support, they are often forced to bear this burden in silence.

The impact of menstrual stigma and the lack of understanding surrounding menstrual health are painfully illustrated by the experiences of the women closest to me. My own mother, who is no longer with us, often expressed a deep sense of anguish at the burden of being born female, likening it to a lifetime of suffering.

One of the most inspiring developments in the fight against menstrual stigma and suffering has been the emergence of grassroots organizations and initiatives led by young women themselves. The Pinkishe Foundation, a youth-led organization dedicated to promoting menstrual health awareness and advocacy, is a shining example of this kind of activism. I had the privilege of learning about the Pinkishe Foundation's work through my niece, Dr. Gudly Nanda, who served as a co-author and editor for an article on their blog.

Premenstrual Syndrome (PMS) is a prime example of a menstrual health issue that is often misunderstood and under-addressed. PMS encompasses a range of physical, psychological, and behavioral symptoms that can occur in the days leading up to menstruation, including mood swings, anxiety, depression, fatigue, and physical discomfort. For some individuals, these symptoms can be severe enough to interfere with daily functioning and quality of life. Research suggests that hormonal fluctuations and neurotransmitter imbalances, particularly in serotonin levels, may play a significant role.

Effective management of PMS often involves a combination of lifestyle changes, such as regular exercise, stress reduction techniques, and dietary modifications, as well as medical interventions like hormonal therapies or anti-inflammatory medications. However, access to these treatments and support systems remains limited for many individuals, particularly those from marginalized communities or lower socioeconomic backgrounds.

Initiatives like paid menstrual leave policies and community-based organizations like the Pinkishe Foundation are helping to break down barriers and create a more inclusive and compassionate society. Ultimately, the fight for menstrual justice is about recognizing the fundamental humanity and dignity of all those who menstruate. It is about creating a world where no one has to suffer in silence or shame, and where access to quality menstrual healthcare is treated as a basic human right.

In the Odia calendar, it is said that there are thirteen festivals in twelve months, highlighting the abundance of celebrations and observances that punctuate the year. However, upon closer examination, there is a darker side to some of these traditional practices. Many of our festivals fail to acknowledge and celebrate the immense contributions and sacrifices made by the women in our families. Savitri Brata, in particular, is a prime example of this inequity. On this day, married women are expected to observe fasts and perform rituals to pray for the longevity and well-being of their husbands.

These customs, while well-intentioned, perpetuate a patriarchal worldview that positions women as dependent on men for their safety and security. It is disheartening to see that even in the 21st century, we continue to adhere to traditions that fail to recognize the strength, resilience, and autonomy of women. The idea that an elder sister should seek protection from her younger brother, rather than being celebrated as a protector herself, is particularly troubling.

Our society has undergone significant transformations in recent decades, moving away from the conservative norms that once defined gender roles and family structures. Today, many women are highly educated and financially independent, with successful careers outside the home. They have become integral contributors to their families' economic stability and well-being, challenging the traditional notion of men as the sole providers.

Women's contributions extend to all aspects of family life. They often take the lead in overseeing their children's education, ensuring that they have the support and resources they need to succeed academically. Despite these significant contributions, women are still often expected to adhere to traditional cultural practices that can be deeply patriarchal and oppressive. Festivals like Savitri Brata, which focus on women's subservience to their husbands, can feel like a slap in the face to women who have worked so hard to achieve equality and independence.

Instead of expecting women to unilaterally pledge their devotion and obedience to their husbands, we should reimagine Savitri Brata as a celebration of equal partnership and mutual respect within marriage. Just as Savitri's love and commitment to Satyavan gave her the strength to face even the god of death, a true partnership is one where both individuals are dedicated to supporting and uplifting each other, through all of life's challenges.

As we move forward, let us reimagine Savitri Brata not as a rigid set of rituals and obligations but as an opportunity for personal reflection and growth. Rather than measuring a woman's devotion by her willingness to fast or perform certain rites, let us encourage both partners to focus on cultivating the qualities of love, respect, and equal commitment that are the true hallmarks of a strong and healthy relationship. For women, this may mean using the occasion of Savitri Brata to reconnect with their own inner strength and wisdom, drawing inspiration from the goddess Savitri's courage and determination.

For men, honoring the spirit of Savitri Brata could mean taking a more active role in supporting and uplifting their partners, both emotionally and practically. It may involve challenging traditional gender roles and expectations and working towards a more equitable division of household responsibilities and decision-making power.

I will always cherish the memory of that day when my younger daughter, despite her tender age, was honored as the best orator at the Kalinga Book Fair Mahotsav at Bhubaneswar, a city renowned for its ancient temples on India's east coast. During the felicitation ceremony, amidst the gathered audience, I had the pleasure of meeting Professor Kulamani Jena, an esteemed poet and author who graciously invited my daughter and me to visit his book stall, Pustak Andolan.

It was during this visit that Prof. Jena introduced me to books addressing various social issues, including those related to the LGBTQ+ community. Terms like "lesbian" and "gay" stood out, challenging my preconceived notions and exposing the gaps in my understanding. Having been conditioned by societal biases to view these words as taboo or immoral, I am ashamed to admit that I initially questioned the author's character and intentions. However, looking back, I realize that my reaction was a reflection of my own ignorance and the deep-rooted prejudices instilled by a society that often marginalizes and stigmatizes individuals based on their sexual orientation or gender identity.

Since that eye-opening encounter, I have made a conscious effort to broaden my perspectives and deepen my understanding of the struggles faced by marginalized communities. I have sought out books, articles, and discussions that shed light on the lived experiences of LGBTQ+ individuals, recognizing the urgent need for greater acceptance, equality, and inclusion in our society. Moreover, I am deeply grateful for the ongoing support and encouragement of Prof. Jena, who has taken a keen interest in my own literary pursuits.

In our society, gender is often viewed through a binary lens, with male and female being the most recognized categories, typically based on a person's anatomy at birth. However, the reality is that gender is a complex and multifaceted spectrum, encompassing a diverse range of identities and expressions that extend far beyond the simplistic notion of a binary.

Transgender individuals are those whose gender identity or expression does not align with the sex they were assigned at birth. This disconnect between one's internal sense of self and their external physical characteristics can lead to a profound sense of discomfort, known as gender dysphoria. Sexual orientation, on the other hand, refers to an individual's emotional, romantic, and/or sexual attraction to others. Lesbian women are those who experience romantic and sexual attraction to other women, while gay men are attracted to other men. Bisexual individuals have the capacity for romantic and sexual attraction to both men and women.

The term "queer" has evolved over time to become an inclusive umbrella term for all gender and sexual minorities. Once used as a derogatory slur, it has been reclaimed by the LGBTQ+ community as a positive self-descriptor, embodying a sense of pride and resistance against societal norms. Pride parades and marches are vibrant outdoor events that serve as both a celebration of LGBTQ+ identity and a platform for advocacy and protest. These gatherings bring together lesbian, gay, bisexual, transgender, and queer individuals, along with their allies, to promote social acceptance, fight for legal rights, and showcase the community's achievements and resilience.

One powerful example of the ongoing struggle for LGBTQ+ acceptance and equality is the story of Indian sprinter Dutee Chand, who made headlines last year when she publicly revealed that she was in a same-sex relationship. Despite facing significant backlash and discrimination in the wake of her announcement, Dutee remains undaunted in her commitment to living her truth. She acknowledges that her revelation has changed the way some people view her but refuses to let others' opinions define her or diminish her sense of self-worth. Instead, she uses her platform to encourage others in same-sex relationships to be courageous, stand firm in their identities, and resist the pressure to hide or conform to societal expectations.

As we work towards building a more inclusive and equitable society, it is crucial that we listen to and amplify the voices of LGBTQ+ individuals like Dutee Chand. By creating spaces for open dialogue, challenging our own biases and assumptions, and actively supporting the rights and well-being of gender and sexual minorities, we can foster a culture of understanding, respect, and celebration of diversity in all its forms.

You may be wondering why I have chosen to delve into the complex and often misunderstood topic of gender diversity and the LGBTQ+ community. My journey of learning and understanding began when I inadvertently overheard a frank discussion between my daughters and nieces about their own gender identities and sexual orientations. As they shared their thoughts and experiences with each other, I found myself intrigued and eager to learn more about these concepts that were, admittedly, foreign to me at the time.

Driven by a desire to better understand and support my loved ones, I embarked on a personal quest for knowledge. I turned to online resources, seeking out information and perspectives on the diverse range of gender identities and expressions that exist beyond the binary of male and female. At first, I struggled to grasp the nuances and complexities of these issues, as they challenged many of the assumptions and norms I had grown up with. However, I refused to let my initial confusion or discomfort deter me from learning and growing.

Through open and honest conversations with my daughters, I began to develop a deeper understanding and appreciation for the richness and diversity of human identity and experience. I learned about the challenges and discrimination faced by LGBTQ+ individuals and the importance of creating safe and inclusive spaces where everyone can feel valued and respected for who they are. This journey of learning and understanding has been a humbling and transformative experience for me. It has required me to confront my own biases and limitations and to cultivate a deeper sense of empathy, compassion, and respect for those whose identities and experiences differ from my own.

As I continue on this path of learning and growth, I am committed to using my voice and platform to raise awareness, challenge injustice, and advocate for the rights and dignity of all individuals, regardless of their gender identity or sexual orientation. Ultimately, my hope is that by fostering a culture of openness, respect, and celebration of diversity, we can create a world where every individual can live authentically and without fear of discrimination or violence. It is a vision that requires ongoing work and dedication from all of us, but one that I believe is both necessary and achievable.

So let us continue to engage in these critical conversations, to educate ourselves and others, and to stand in solidarity with the LGBTQ+ community. Together, we can build a society that truly embraces and values the full spectrum of human identity and experience, and that ensures that every individual can live with dignity, equality, and pride.

THE POOL

Nick Garlick

It was the tail end of summer and Alex was alone when he found the pool. He was staying with some friends in a cottage on a small island off the coast of Croatia. Well, not his friends. He hadn't even met them until he'd turned up at Stansted to take the flight out. The only person he knew in the group was the girl he'd met three weeks before and who he'd been fucking regularly ever since.

He'd never been to Croatia, but he'd heard good things about it and had always been curious. And it really hadn't been all that hard to talk this new girl into inviting him along. One good, hard, extra attentive fuck and she'd practically begged him to accompany her. Of course, he'd had to pay his own air fare, but he'd been able to borrow that from his regular girlfriend without her asking too many questions. And once he was on the island and in the cottage, regular shagging each night was enough to ensure that the twit he'd come with would pay for everything else.

It wasn't too hard a price to pay, he thought. Not so he could cross Croatia off his list of places to visit. And it was only for eight nights. After that he'd be back in London and wouldn't have to see her again. Because as spectacular as her tits were, and as hot and tight as her cunt was, everything else about her was beginning to bore *his* tits off. Christ, she'd even talked about introducing him to her parents!

Not that she'd talked about it for long. He'd just done what he usually did when a girl started using her mouth to spout all sorts of daft bollocks. He'd stuck his cock in it and given her something else to think about instead. That usually worked. He had a good cock and a good body and there wasn't a lot he had to do with them – to get girls to do what he wanted - except get them both naked.

The ones that approach didn't work with – and there weren't too many of them, he could guarantee you that – he just never saw again. Life was too short to waste on talking lesbians out of their clothes.

So anyway, there he was on a hot and sunny afternoon, taking a walk by himself in the woods behind the cottage the twit's friends had rented. They'd gone off after lunch, wanting to see some site of, in their words, *historical significance*. Which struck Alex as about as much fun as cutting a corpse's toenails. Besides, he'd just given the twit an extra-long fuck before lunch and he was tired. He needed a nap. So they went off, he slept, and when he woke up and it was still hours to go before anyone got back and started cooking supper, he decided he might as well pass the time by looking around.

Who knew? He might see something of *historical significance*.

Which he did in the end, but only by accident, and only because he didn't like being told what to do by anyone, let alone a wrinkly old bag in walking boots.

He met her ten minutes after he'd left the cottage. She was coming up the path towards him and he heard her before he saw her, talking on her mobile. He could tell she was old by her voice, and the last thing he wanted to do was talk to an *old* woman.

Different story if it had been a girl in a bikini with nice tits. Might even have even have been able to chat her up enough to get her to get those tits out and give him a blow job. He'd done it before. Several times.

But it wasn't a girl in a bikini with nice tits, so when he saw a gap in the undergrowth to his left, he slipped away into it to avoid the oncoming walker. Only trouble was, he didn't do it fast enough and she saw him. 'Not a good idea,' she called out.

The warning intrigued Alex just enough to slow him down. Which gave the old biddy enough time to catch up to him and shake her head. 'It can be dangerous in there,' she said.

She had an accent. Croatian? Not that Alex cared. He was too busy taking in her big old boobs and stringy legs and thinking she might once have been worth a shag. But not now. No fucking way.

'What's dangerous about it?' he asked.

'There's a pool.'

'A pool?'

'Yes, a pool. To swim in.'

'So what's wrong with that? Is it private?'

'No,' said the woman. 'But something bad happened there, a long time ago, and the woman who built it, as a memorial, was... disturbed.'

'Sounds like an old horror film on telly,' Alex said, smiling his sexy seductive smile. He couldn't help himself. He was talking to a female - even if she was old – and it was automatic.

The woman smiled back, but it wasn't a smile with a lot of humour in it. 'I suppose it does,' she agreed. 'But really, you shouldn't go in there. You –' Alex was getting bored. And he didn't like the way she was staring at him. Made him think of his mother, that domineering old cunt, who'd never stopped ordering him around for one fucking second in his whole fucking life. 'Well, thanks for the advice,' he said, 'but I'm a big boy. I can look after myself.'

And with that he turned and set off through the trees, brushing aside a branch so loudly he didn't hear the woman's parting words.

'Yes. That's what big boys always say.'

On he walked, along a path that grew narrower and narrower and more and more choked with vegetation. The only thing that kept him going was being told he shouldn't but, even so, he was right on the point of giving up when he pushed a final branch aside and stepped into a scene of wonder. Wonder even for Alex.

Before him, in the middle of a patch of bare open ground, was a large, oval-shaped pool of water, edged with curved stone panels. They were pale pink, warm to the touch and as smooth as marble. The water, still and flat, was even warmer. It tasted ever so slightly salty.

It was deep, too. He could see no bottom, even though the water was a clear clean blue that let him peer down far into the depths. The sides of the pool, apparently built of the same pink stone as the edging, seemed to go on forever, fading away into the distance.

He blinked and shook his head. As he did so, he noticed a few sentences carved deep into the stones and spaced evenly around the perimeter of the pool. They were in English and easy to read.

Things that happened aren't forgotten.

Someone always remembers

To set things right.

Eventually.

Whatever the fuck that meant, Alex thought, when he'd read every word. Not that it was any weirder than the rest of the place. The old biddy had told him the pool had been built a long time ago and that was obviously bollocks. It looked like it had been built yesterday. The stones gleamed, the water was as clean as if it had just been poured and the ground *around* the pool was flat and free of weeds.

Old? Alex thought. *Definitely bollocks!*

He straightened up and stripped off his clothes. He wasn't wearing any underwear – he rarely did – and as he unzipped his jeans his cock flopped into view. It was big, even when not erect, and always got stares on nude beaches. For one brief moment he thought he was being watched and turned around to face the way he'd come in, thinking that if that woman had followed him, he'd give her some-thing to gurgle about over her late-night cup of cocoa. But there was nobody there. And he couldn't actually see *where* he'd come in. The shrubs and trees now seemed to form an impenetrable wall of green. Problem for later, he thought as he kicked off his jeans and plunged into the water.

It was so warm that once he surfaced he had to blink and shake his head to be sure he'd actually landed *in* water. There was no difference whatsoever between *his* body temperature and the con-tents of the pool. Definitely salty, though, which made him wonder where its source lay. The sea? A hot spring further inland?

Well, wherever it came from, it was pleasure to swim in and for the next fifteen minutes he drifted happily back and forth, pushing

himself this way and that, luxuriating in the warmth and the still-
ness of his surroundings.

It was when he was making one more gentle turn and thinking
about getting out that he spotted movement below him. Or at least,
he thought he did. He couldn't be sure what it was he'd seen, and
when he ducked his head under the surface for another look, he
saw nothing but the smooth blank walls of the pool, stretching
away into darkness.

Probably just a reflection, he thought. On the surface. The after-
noon sun was fading now, slipping away behind the trees, casting
shadows on the clearing and the pool. Must have been that. Even
so, he felt ever so faintly uneasy and decided it was time to leave
and head back home.

Except he couldn't.

The stones that ran round the rim of the pool were wider than
he'd thought, and rounded, and no matter how hard he tried, he
couldn't quite reach the far edge to get a grip and pull himself out.
His hands kept slipping free.

At first he thought this was because his fingers were wet. So he
drifted back and forth for a while, with both arms held up out of
the water to get them dry – which didn't take long in the afternoon
heat – and then tried again.

Still no luck. Dry hands or wet, he could find no purchase on
the stone. Nor could he get a grip with his toes on the sides of
the pool and use that as leverage. It was too smooth. His feet kept
slipping loose.

He was stuck.

And he had no idea how he was going to get out.

He paddled back and forth for a few minutes, then began to shout. 'Is anybody there? Can anybody help me? I'm stuck!'

His cries echoed in the clearing and died away to silence.

'I'm in the pool!' he yelled. 'I can't get *out*!

His voice broke on the last word and he choked as water slopped into his mouth. He spat it out and hurled himself at the rim. He put every ounce of energy he could summon into the lunge and for one ever-so-brief moment felt his finger tips touch the far edge of the stone.

Only to come loose and send him sliding back.

And there he stayed, treading water, calling out again and again in an ever-hoarser voice to rescuers who never came. The sun faded, the sky darkened and soon new shadows fell across the surface of the pool as the full moon rose above the trees and cast its light on the clearing.

As it did so, Alex felt something he'd rarely felt before.

Fear.

He wasn't cold – the water was as warm as ever and showed no signs of losing any heat to the night air – but he *was* tired. And that was what was making him scared. Because he didn't know how long he could go on staying afloat, keeping his head above water. Already he'd felt the first faint twinges of a cramp, a cramp he'd managed to dismiss with a few vigorous rubs of his calf. But he had no doubt it would return at some point. And no doubt harsher and more deadly.

Then what?

He couldn't believe this was happening. How could he end up stuck like this? Who could have built such a fucking stupid pool in the first place, a swimming pool you couldn't get out of? What was the point of *that*, for fuck's sake?

Then, as a new wave of panic flooded through him, three things happened in close succession.

A fresh cramp struck, and not just the calf this time but the whole leg from ankle to thigh. The pain made him cry out loud, a cry cut off in a panicky gurgle as he stopped treading water and his head sank below the surface.

He came back up spitting and coughing. As he did so, he noticed a light beneath him.

A light?

In spite of the pain he could see it clearly, far below, no more than a pinprick really. But as he watched, in between gulps of air and frantic leg massaging, he saw it widen and grow, expanding until it filled the bottom of the pool.

Which he could now *also* see clearly. A smooth flat bottom constructed of the same pale pink stone as the rest of the pool.

And moving.

It was definitely moving, swaying from side to side and parting – yes, parting – in the middle.

What the *fuck*, he thought, was happening?

Then there was no time to think any further because he was having to struggle to keep his head in the air. He couldn't kick hard enough with his one good leg and he couldn't use his arms because he needed them to try to massage the cramp away. Choking and gagging, his head slipped under once again and the pain in his leg was like a jagged spike ripping through his body from his foot to his skull.

He surged back up, screaming now, screaming in fear and frustration and agony, screaming so loud he was sure somebody had to hear him. They couldn't *not* hear him.

And for one brief second, as he flailed wildly about, he was sure he glimpsed a figure standing at the edge of the clearing. It was the old woman who'd warned him not to go down the path to the pool.

But she wasn't moving towards him. She was standing quite still. Watching.

He tried calling out to her, but the only sound he produced was a choked off gasp as his head went under yet again and water filled his lungs. And this time he couldn't do anything to stop himself sinking. The pain in his leg was too intense and he just didn't have the energy to struggle any more. He was going to drown, and he knew it.

The thought petrified him.

But as he sank on downwards, he saw something that wiped the fear from his mind and replaced it with a terror he'd never believed possible. Because he'd seen what had been moving at the bottom of the pool. He could see what was waiting for him.

A mouth.

A mouth as wide as the pool itself and with teeth, he knew, as sharp and merciless as razors.

COOPERS ROCK-MAN

Andi Stout

Out of kindling, burlap, moss,
and mud brick, students created him.
Nose bulbous—content,
he naps against a tree,
like a Rip Van Winkle totem,
fingers laced, green beard stretching
the arc of his portly stomach.
Maybe he's dreaming

of summer weekends spent lounging
in a hammock tied between two Sugar Maples
in the backyard he and his wife can't yet afford,
instead of working to make ends almost meet.
Maybe he's dreaming

of drinking hot cocoa fireside
with his children on a snow day—
home from school—telling family stories
about how he put his eldest's crib together
by flashlight in a storm much worse,
instead of braving blizzards at 5 AM
to get the kids to the sitter's by 6,
work by 7:15

because the Family Leave Act of '93
doesn't cover contingent positions.

I wonder if the forest faeries will reward him,
wake him after a revolution in an era
where working-class
doesn't mean working all the time.

CHARUMBIRA, IT'S A NUDE AND NOTORIOUS GENOCIDE

Ndaba Sibanda

This is a big and bare fiasco and farce.
How is it not a genocide, Charumbira?
Do you ever empathize and sympathize?

Are you going to be so conscienceless,
deceitful, careless and heartless so that
your disgraceful and driveling denial
possibly prospers in burying, brutalizing,
deleting, discoloring, distorting and duping
historical evidence: facts and figures forever?

How? At least try to get real, if not sleek!
How is it not a genocide, Charumbira,
when the myriad shallow graves are in grief,
when the innocent were slain in great numbers,
in a deliberate way and with the aim or intent
to destroy that nation or group in whole or part,
when the scale and facts speak for themselves,
when the apt terminology and definition exist,
when the helpless victims and the survivors
are still nursing genocidal, psychological
emotional and social scars and wounds?

How can you have genocidal victims
and survivors on one hand,
and on the other, no genocide?
Charumbira ponder Ubuntu. Repent.
Cruel, crude lies like these tend to haunt.

That you don't grasp the right classification
does not only qualify you to be disqualified,
but it also behooves the world and peacemakers
not to stand by as you seek to demolish the word
from usage for the fear of heinous crimes perpetrated
by those who wanted to rout innocent and unarmed souls.
The truth is that it is a genocide, it will never be anything else.
I mean you and your mean partners in crime know and fear it.

You can wish and try as much as you want:
the bitter truth is that now the world knows
about the Gukurahundi genocide and the pranks,
dismal delays and denials of the Gukurahundists,
beneficiaries and their circles of friends and fans.

If anything such a blatant statement that is devoid
of decency, direction, honesty and truth has bellied you
and your partners in crime that this 'process' has nothing
to do with truth-telling, healing, closure, human rights,
and the plight of the survivors and relatives but is a skewed,
unsympathetic and sick sham that has everything to do with
the protection and perfuming of the powerful perpetrators,
the privileged heirs, toadies and backhanders of the system,
and the eternal evaders of justice, truth-telling and transparency.
Why are journalists barred from covering the hearing sessions?

Deputy president of the Chiefs Council,
the chief truth that is that you clearly coasted
away from the bitter truths and cohesion,

yet this stage-managed trickery and foolery
is supposed to be cohesive and truth-telling, right?

By the way, when, where and how did the chiefs,
who are traditional leaders, get the capacity and jurisdiction
to carry out this mammoth task befitting of an international
independent tribunal? Are these community leaders not
compromised as beneficiaries of the system? Where is the
authority of the Constitution in this fracas? How is this
charade victim-centered? Is this not a set fiasco?
Do you expect a sincere rightist, victim or survivor to buy into this
sick scam?

JUSTICE FOR THE PEOPLE

Vanessa Caraveo

The people are tired and hungry.
Days turn into years and still no change.
The rich rule the land full of corruption
never wanting the poor to move up in life.
Oppression is the name of the game.

Those courageous souls brave enough
to raise their voice against such injustice,
end up paying the high price with their life.
Generations go through the same cycle
without a gleam of hope for positive change.

Law enforcement cannot be trusted
for they are easily bought and just as corrupt.
The people can only lean on each other
praying their children have a better future
but realizing the harsh reality that awaits them.

Fortunes the rich have could easily help many
but they choose to waste it on superficial luxuries instead.
Fancy cars, huge houses, brand name apparel
used only to boast and feel superior to their fellow man.
Meanwhile their selfish ego continues to inflate with no end.

The people must unite once and for all
and not let their powerful voices be silenced.
They shall be inspired by Emiliano Zapata's great words,
It is better to die on your feet than live on your knees.
They will persevere for a brighter tomorrow.

For oppression and with fear is no way to live
and something needs to be done for the children.
We are powerful together and will triumph against evil.
We are all equal in God's eyes and deserve to live in peace.
I will never lose hope that there will be justice for the people.

APPARITIONS

John Tavares

Frank encouraged Bettina to obtain an abortion. As a mature student, who faced an uncertain future, after graduation from university at an older than average age, Frank didn't feel assured and prepared.

"Whoever is?" Bettina demanded.

He said he didn't feel confident he'd earn the income to support a mother and child, who faced unlimited challenges. He accepted the job offer from the insurance company, where Bettina had roles as varied as financial analyst, statistician, and economist, although she preferred the term econometrician. He was puzzled the insurance company hired him, until he discovered the unemployed actors and idle artists who worked in sales and on commission. Still, Frank wasn't confident he would last in his position as a claims adjuster. So, he discussed with her the need for an abortion. Frank explained he never expected he'd get a woman pregnant, even inadvertently, especially a co-worker.

Bettina emphasized they worked in separate departments and subsidiaries. She earned far more money than him as a high-ranking executive, not a company foot soldier. She considered Frank more a friend with benefits and didn't believe they dated in the conventional sense. Their relationship she considered spontaneous, not platonic, and the sex nothing more than a one-night stand, although previously she considered him a close friend.

Disappointed in their relationship, they took long walks, along Bloor Street, the boardwalk through the Beaches and the shoreline of Lake Ontario, and through High Park, while they conversed at length and in depth. When she sensed his worry and even dread, she realized an infant would not keep them bonded as a couple. Bettina committed herself to an abortion.

"Commitment—now there's an unfamiliar word in your vocabulary. Remember that term of endearment; it might come in handy someday."

Still, she reassured him she would follow through with an abortion, but he said she should do whatever she thought best. She allowed him to accompany her to the appointments with the gynecologist. During the visit to the sterile, smooth, antiseptic offices, he constantly asked about her condition. She felt nothing but coldness and emptiness, when the gynecologist slipped the jellied surgical instruments inside her and scraped her uterus, as she suffered complications. Afterwards, Frank was ready to call a taxi, but she stoically insisted on taking the subway train home. He walked her home from the subway station. When he asked her if she wanted him to stay and brew her tea or coffee and have some cookies or muffins, Bettina said she had none. "Do you have cookies and muffins at home?" she queried.

He admitted he had no cookies and muffins in his food pantry, which was barren, except for the containers of coffee and tea and cans of tuna fish he stockpiled from the dollar and wholesale discount store. She replied this was a reason they could not have children. He couldn't provide and assume responsibility for children, she said. Frank agreed he was irresponsible and couldn't find that job he could call a career or profession. He was happy to live a quiet, thrifty life, without the distractions and responsibilities of children.

Bettina insisted they visit Trinity Bellwoods Park, which they had toured several times before. They made the trip to the park on a weekend. He read, while Bettina tried to picnic. Then she tanned in the sun that shimmered in the park and napped on a beach blanket. When she woke, he was reading a newspaper. She drank a beer and a vodka cooler and tried to persuade him to have a hard seltzer. As dusk approached, she said they needed to escape the dislocation and desolation of small apartments, the Internet, smartphones, even the social isolation and distancing of the pandemic. She insisted they both imbibe hallucinogenic mushrooms.

Seeing how she suffered through an abortion, as a sign of support for her, he agreed to take the psychedelic mushrooms she saved for experimentation. She found a suitable quiet place in the park. She spread a blanket down on the grass and insisted that they assume the lotus position. She gave him a chilled, sweating tall can and asked, "Did you bring me apple cider?" "Sorry, I didn't," Frank replied.

"How could we have had a baby, if you can't bring me an apple cider?" Bettina asked. "I don't think you could ever be a provider."

Frank agreed she had a salient point. This is why, he believed, she took the correct action in having an abortion.

She gave him a magic mushroom, after she chewed and swallowed one herself. He placed the dried, withered mushroom in his mouth, like it was the wafer of the Holy Communion of the Catholic church. He slowly consumed the mushroom, remembering the panic attacks he experienced in the past when he took a blotter of LSD. So, she advised this was not a clever idea—contraindicated was the term she sought—but he insisted. He admitted he feared he would experience yet another bad trip, like the greenout he had when he took cannabis gummies, yet he imbibed the mushroom, which sat on his tongue while they argued. He felt he owed her some form of sacrifice, some trip outside his comfort zone, after she experienced the trauma and ordeal of an abortion.

Then Frank drank the second apple cider she offered him. They listened to the chill, mellow Chinese classical music she played in the wireless speaker from her smartphone. She asked him how he felt. He said he felt normal, even though he saw scintillating lights. He said he felt nothing but emptiness.

Did he understand? Bettina asked abruptly.

He said he understood, but he felt disoriented and confused.

Afterwards, Bettina did not hear from him for weeks. He returned to work as an insurance adjuster, examining claims and documentation, including videos and photos of fire and storm damaged houses, methodically following the procedures to evaluate replacement costs and calculate expenses. And he endlessly commuted and travelled on the subway train, streetcars, and buses, between offices and work sites.

When Frank boarded the subway train and saw the doors slide shut, he saw the figure of a child. He saw the heartbreak and disappointment of the boy as he failed to board the subway train before it sped off, leaving him behind forever.

Then, at lunch break, he decided to skip his favorite Chinese restaurant for the decadence of a hot dog from the food cart vendor.

As he took his first bite of the hot dog, he saw the same visage of the child peering at him hungrily. He dropped the hot dog and spilled the condiments of relish, ketchup, and mustard on his seat, and the vision of the child disappeared.

Later, Frank went to the gym in the community recreation center, attached to the public library, and shot hoops in the basket-ball court. Again, the child appeared to him, but this time in a t-shirt, gym shorts, and sneakers. The child looked at him forlornly and rubbed his eyes. When he finally shot a basket, a three pointer, the child disappeared.

When Frank went to his favorite branch of the public library, which he liked because their patrons were usually adults, with no children, he looked up. He saw the child glance up at him. At the circulation desk, though, when he started to argue with the librarian over a missing book, an overdue movie DVD, and overdue fees, the child disappeared.

Later, Bettina called him again on her cellphone. She invited him to Woodbine Beach for an evening session of yoga and a skinny dip on the night of the summer solstice. Skinny dipping was a favorite edgy urban adventure, aside from nude yoga and happy endings in the sauna. Despite the fair weather, the beach was virtually abandoned.

Bettina insisted they take mushrooms. Frank was inclined to say no, but the potential for insight and altered states of conscious-ness, leading to enlightenment, if he imbibed the mushrooms, now seemed worth the risk. After he swallowed his magic mushrooms, Bettina took more psilocybin. She started to chant and read aloud from the *Tibetan Book of the Dead* as the beach became engulfed in darkness. She lit a candle and played music and chimes and drum-ming from Buddhist musicians.

"You plied me with drink, when normally you don't drink."

As the accusatory tone and accusations from her grew, Frank warned her she seemed under the influence of psychedelics, but still the recriminations continued. "Bettina, you brought the tequila. When you called me your cabana boy and asked, I poured. I should have cut you off, but I'm not a bartender. I'm not a good judge of sobriety."

"What was it about me that was such an allure. Was it my shapely body and large breasts?"

"You're putting me in an awkward position," Frank said.

"Then when my judgment was impaired, and my defenses were down, you had your way with me, and fucked me."

"I did nothing without your consent."

"But I was in no position—"

"You put yourself into that position, didn't you? You wanted to be in a mental state where you would make rash and bad decisions with impunity. You wanted to act impulsively, spontaneously. That is what you wanted. Wasn't that a bit manipulative?"

"You took advantage of my impaired judgement. You got me pregnant and put me through the nightmare of an abortion."

Frank tried to get Bettina to notice the beauty of the beach at nighttime, but to her it was a vast empty chasm. He observed the place should have been crowded at this time with the transcendence of the summer solstice. Instead, a sprinkling of rain earlier that evening discouraged city dwellers from the summons of nature.

Frank remained mute, silent, but, when she tossed the rest of her hard seltzer at him, he said, "I can see there's no sense or rationality in arguing with you."

He followed her through the darkness after she slipped off her summer dress, her bra, and panties. He took off his cargo shorts, t-shirt, and sandals, and followed her to the shoreline. Bettina slipped into the water, waded deep, and swam far from shore into Lake Ontario at Woodbine Beach. Frank followed her from the undulating shoreline and the sandy beach, in the darkness, the en-compassing blackness, despite her fear of the open lake and chilly water. When Bettina emerged from the lake, having swum out to the buoy, she was alone. She called out to him in the immense dark abyss of Lake Ontario, an inland freshwater sea. But he failed to reply, and she could not observe him swimming or splashing through the darkness and blackness. She could not detect him, could see no sign of him, no sign of life, in the lake. Bettina dressed on the sandy beach, realizing as she glanced towards the lights that surrounded the massive concrete structure of the diving tower and outdoors swimming pools and the abandoned police storefront, she had been taking a chance swimming nude. She gathered her handbag, sandals, and belongings, and strode along the boardwalk, until she reached the swimming pool. She walked along the side-walk beneath the concrete complex to the bus stop. She caught a late-night bus past Queen Street East, lined with pubs, cafes, shops, and restaurants, to Woodbine subway station. When she arrived at her stop she walked home. Meanwhile, after drifting far from the shoreline, in the darkness, in a state of suspended animation, and sensory deprivation, he eventually swam to shore, shivering from nudity, exposure, the cold.

On Mother's Day, filled with a strange sense of dread and foreboding, he double checked the batteries, functions, and working order of his carbon monoxide monitor and smoke detector. He even conducted a quick test of the detectors, triggering an ear-piercing alarm, which immediately aroused complaints and thumps and knocks from neighboring apartments. He also prepared for Mother's Day by doing things he normally never did on a Sunday: he woke early, before sunrise; he left his apartment before noon. He went out with the hobbyist tool his sister condemned: his camera. He decided he would take a random walk, whilst pursuing his hobby of photography, which his sister loathed, particularly his street photography. Urbana could never understand why he would want to take candid photographs of random strangers in an urban setting; she could never perceive any use for his photography or any artistic merit in his pursuit. His sister denounced his activity and considered his behavior inappropriate.

Frank decided he would fight back against the haunting apparitions and images he experienced of Urbana, who functioned as a mother to him, since their mother, a single parent, often left care of the far younger sibling, to her daughter.

His sister and mother died on Mother's Day, under mysterious circumstances, in the family home. The coroner determined the cause of death was carbon monoxide poisoning. The fire marshal's investigation determined the chimney for the wood stove had been blocked. The investigators who combed thoroughly through the house and examined the wood stove and pipes suspected the chimney had been deliberately blocked. After these findings, the police deemed their deaths suspicious. They suspected foul play, but their investigations uncovered no further evidence. His mother certainly didn't have the strength or will, since she was recovering from a heart attack.

Frank rode the subway downtown. As soon as he stepped into the Sam the Record Man store, he could hear his sister's voice of retribution and condemnation. (Urbana became a born again Christian with her last boyfriend. But he broke up with her when he moved to the United States to attend a religious vocational college and married a Mormon.) As he bought a vintage Rolling Stones album from the sixties, he heard Urbana denounce Mick Jagger. Frank could hear the harsh tones of Urbana denouncing the evil music, urging him to turn down the rock and roll or she would throw his ghetto blaster out the door. The voice of Urbana was severe, condemnatory.

He skipped his original plans to head to a café to savor a cappuccino and read the remastered album's liner notes. Instead, he headed across the city to the library at the Ontario Institute for Studies in Education. The daycare had recently taken into its custody and care a child with a severe case of autism. Frank remained committed to personally learning more about the condition.

As he walked the aisles of the library, in search of the appropriate monograph, he could hear his sister condemning his habit of reading and book collecting. He should pursue manly Canadian interests like hockey, ice fishing, snowshoeing. She liked when he hunted snowshoe hare, ruffed grouse, and moose. She wanted him to take the chain saw and cut firewood, since she loved to cook with the woodstove and cherished the heat and warmth the fire radiated during a frigid northern winter. She enjoyed driving a pickup truck down logging roads and gathering firewood with him. His sister praised the rural lifestyle and outdoorsman's life. He explored nature and the outdoors as an adolescent and teenager in northwestern Ontario—the lifestyle he abandoned when he moved to southern Ontario to attend university. She insisted he should read more books like the Bible, and not that profligate, apostasy-spewing, atheist Bertrand Russell.

Frank forgot about the psychology books in a bookshelf, after he came across a woman, aisles over in the stacks, who looked like his sister. The resemblance was so uncanny he even took several photographs. When the woman saw him pointing his camera, she turned away in dismay and disgust, as would his sister. When he checked the memory card, he discovered the images failed to record properly. The camera indicated the digital file was corrupt. The view screen showed only a blurred, out of focus ghostly movement in the photographs, with haloes of light. Frank became even more convinced these images captured his sister's ghostly apparition. Impulsively, Frank decided to visit the spot in Marie Curtis Park where a year ago his friend and coworker hanged himself. He strolled briskly across the campus of the University of Toronto downtown to the Saint George subway station.

He first met Robert through Bettina. She dated Robert until she realized he was more attracted to men. Robert told Bettina something she never forgot: He said certain aspects of her personality disturbed him; at times, he received the impression she derived pleasure from emotionally hurting people. Robert recommended Bettina see a psychiatrist and even set up an appointment with a friend, who practiced from a clinic in a University Avenue hospital. The psychiatrist interviewed her, and, after a few sessions, he diagnosed her with borderline personality disorder. At first, Bettina rejected the diagnosis, dismissing the label and the psychiatrist, cancelling her next appointment. Bettina stopped consulting the psychiatrist completely, thinking he might be Robert's lackey. Later, though, Bettina believed there was more than a kernel of truth to his professional opinion. She also thought Robert should have visited his psychiatrist friend on a professional basis. Robert was conducting research into training and learning techniques utilized by the developmentally disabled before he ended his own existence.

Now Frank decided to visit the scene where Robert struggled and gasped his last breath, but the morbid nature of his outing filled him with foreboding. Still, he felt the need to commemorate his friend and memorialize his memory on the anniversary of his death. He rode the subway train to Kipling Station and then the southbound bus to the lakeshore, where he walked the boulevard paths to the beach park. He became lost in a network of trails, where the adventurous cruised.

Several times, as he traversed the park, he came across a woman who resembled his own sister and dressed as modestly as her, although his sister dressed revealingly in her teenage years. She slept with anyone with an erect penis, until she had an abortion. The trauma of that experience led her back to the Catholic church of their childhood and school years and then the evangelical church up the street from the family home. Frank could hear her con-demnations, as his sister denounced him for remaining single, for watching adult videos, for failing to marry and have children and live a conventional middle-class life.

Finally, he found the spot where their mutual friend Robert, whom he met through Bettina, when she dated him, hung himself. Someone had carved a peace symbol into the massive tree trunk, and the artwork bled tree sap, which looked like dried semen.

Robert was scheduled to appear in criminal court related to charges he faced after an undercover police officer engaged him and entrapped him into sex at this spot, where he later perished. Robert's lawyer was confident prosecutors or the judge would dis-miss the charges or reduce them to an inconsequential provincial offense or even a bylaw infraction. Instead of facing justice and confronting his accusers, Robert hung himself at the same tree, where he was arrested, where sex constantly took place, as well as a hanging or two a year.

Frank found the huge tree in the thick brush and bush of the park. When he spotted the hang rope dangling from the lower branches, he cringed, but took a few pictures. As he snapped the photographs, he thought he saw several images of his sister, in her grey coat, plaid shirt, and blue jeans, lurking amidst the trees.

He felt overwhelmed with vertigo and decided he needed to leave the park as quickly as possible. He strode quickly along the twisted network of trails through the bushes from the park. He decided to take the Bloor-Danforth subway train back downtown.

The days were longer with the waning of spring and the blossoming of summer. He partook in street photography around Yonge Street near the huge downtown shopping mall and in Nathan's Phillips Square. He photographed colorful characters, the foppish, the punk rockers, the overdressed, the underdressed, the colorful, the conspicuous.

Every time he captured a subject, a woman lurked in the background who reminded him of the presence of his sister. Filled with fear, he cringed, as the voice of his sister, her recrimination, flooded his sensorium and conscience. When he entered Dundas subway station, he could hear her voice of reproach, her urgent plea he end his misery.

Later, police officers investigated, and mental health professionals asked him questions about what happened next, and he provided these answers. As the subway train sped into Dundas station, he even saw Urbana behind the driver's windshield. He felt such a surge of energy he lost his wits and panicked. Fearful he might fall off the platform into the train tracks, he collided with a young woman, who resembled Urbana to an uncanny degree. This university student, returning to her college dormitory following hockey practice and beers at a pub on Queen Street, played hockey. She pushed him, and Frank spun awkwardly, lost his balance and footing, and fell backwards in front of the speeding train.

Bettina learned Frank had been detained on a mental health warrant after that incident. She called him at the hospital on University Avenue in downtown Toronto. The hospital switchboard operator and then a nurse transferred his call to his room, as he rested and recuperated in the psychiatric ward of Mount Sinai Hospital. He said he tried talking with counselors and psychiatrists and fellow patients in group therapy, but he did not feel the talks and sessions were productive. Bettina visited him, she admitted, because she was curious, although she wanted to see if she could help. He confessed to her over the telephone he thought the operator of that subway train resembled his own sister. The train's wheels squealed as she applied the brakes with all her force and as the tons of trains commuters rolled in dangerous proximity. Bettina went to the psychiatric ward in the hospital and visited him in his private room, paid for by his workplace health insurance, he said.

Having returned from the fitness club, where she worked out on the treadmill, the stationary bicycle, and lifted weights, she was dressed in her athletic apparel, black leggings, a crop top, long sleeve shirt, a short-sleeve t-shirt, track pants, and a rainproof jacket, and she carried a gym bag.

"You'll have to teach me the roll."

"The roll?"

"They said it was amazing you survived your fall, or jump, on the subway tracks. They said you knew instinctively what to do and rolled away from the path of the subway train to safety."

"Who are they?" Frank asked.

"Mutual friends."

"These friends—they chose strange times to come out of the woodwork." "You do have friends."

"So, we're friends?"

"Friends, indeed."

"The last time I saw you I thought you left me for dead."

"You've changed, really changed. Last time I saw you were working as an insurance adjuster. Now you're working in early childhood education. That seems an unlikely career move."

"I worked in insurance to pay the rent and bills. For some odd reason, the most stodgy and conservative corporation was the only potential employer willing to take a risk in hiring the person with the most unusual and least impressive resume. Anyway, children bring out the best in me."

"Aren't you worried people will think you're a predator?"

Frank stared at Bettina long and hard, longer and harder than he intended, or even expected, but she had struck a raw nerve. This wasn't the attitude and expression Bettina expected and his reproach felt hurtful. Bettina intended to tell him about the diagnosis of borderline personality disorder she received, but she said, "I'm sorry."

Bettina walked abruptly out of the private room on the ward—sobbing. She passed by the nursing station and the nurse, piqued by curiosity, rushed to his room.

"What happened?" the nurse asked.

Frank shrugged and took a sleeping pill from its paper cup, swallowed it, and took a sip of ice water.

Afterwards, doctors, nurses, and paramedics treated Bettina in the emergency department of the same hospital. When she rushed from the hospital front entrance, she tried to cross the six lanes of traffic on University Avenue in a hurry, sobbing, through traffic and the darkness of a Toronto night downtown. She was struck by speeding traffic, a parcel delivery van, whose driver's acted reflexively and quickly. He loaded her like an expedited express delivery alongside heavy parcels into the back of his truck and sped to the emergency department entrance on the nearby laneway. He rushed through sliding doors and glass foyers, past ambulances and paramedics, into the emergency department, carrying in his arms her injured body, with her broken bones, hemorrhages, and contusions. The emergency doctors and nurses quickly took over. Frank had gone downstairs for coffee from the café and snacks from the vending machine. He noticed her on the gurney downstairs during the commotion, nurses and paramedics scrambling, in the hospital corridor. Afterwards, he visited her in the intensive care unit and trauma ward every day during afternoon and evening visiting hours. Then she finally believed he showed remorse and regret, as she recovered and underwent physical rehabilitation.

IN AMERICA

Cecil Morris

where guns are guaranteed, protected,
semi-automatic thoughts and prayers
fill the air whenever a foreseeable tragedy
comes to pass and common sense is thwarted
in courts by the good man argument about
inalienable right to armor piercing ammo
and high capacity magazines and arms,
lots and lots of arms for self-defense
and hunting and sport and just because
what's right is right and god-given and beyond
all reason. In America we have the right
to kill any and everything that enters
our personal space or would make us back down
or feel discomfort (even a smidgen) unless,
of course, it is an embryo abandoned
in cryogenic storage, a holy seed
of personhood, a sacrosanct singularity
that must be defended until born and then
all bets are off and children are on their own.
In these United States of Guns, where firearms
outnumber arms and kids and arms on kids,
children are fair game. In the shooting galleries
of America—schools, parades, theaters,

shopping malls—they can be targets just the same
as anyone else. Like Vonnegut said
in Slaughterhouse Five, so it goes. At least,
in this post-modern, neocolonial
slow-mo unraveling, apocalyptic world,
our rights are safe, our guns, our homes because
of good people with adequate fire power
unless one of them everyone thought was fine
(or maybe a dangerous menace someone warned
authorities about) becomes a bad person
and starts shooting up the innocent and launches
another round of thoughts and prayers into our air.

STRANGE WORLD

Adriana Rocha

We all
Work a lot,
We live in
The same neighborhood,
We try to speak
The same language
But what we earn
Varies,
Some can buy
Themselves expensive
Shoes and others
Just food.

INALEINABLE

Joseph E. Arechavala

inalienable rights
but not for savage Indians
or those Chinamen
not for the women
who birthed them
not for chained and beaten
created equal
but not equal
intellectual dishonesty
is easy
reality defiles words
especially the most noble words
we are still
yet to embrace
those words
carefully
written so very long ago

NATURE NURTURES UNCONDITIONALLY

Mohammad Haseen Ahmed

Nature nurtures unconditionally and offers solace unsolicited,
Under its benign influence it nourishes your body, mind and soul
    without asking who you are, unintended
Whereas we humans always tend to discriminate against each other
    unperturbed,
When the sun shines for all, the rain quenches the thirst of every
    parched land, pours on every dry seed to germinate,
Roses, jasmines and lotus blossom and look awesome for all
    mankind,
Why we humans prowl to put others at peril and our Consciences
    remain unpricked,
Mother nature embrace us all, give comforts and coziness without
    ever being biased,
Let's take a leaf out of it and plant a seed of fraternity and equality
    leaving all animosity behind

EXODUS

Rob Rolfe

(Part of *Gaza Poems*)

the new
nakba
has begun

an unholy
exodus
of trucks

children
exhausted
families

nowhere
to go
but into

the dark
heart
of hell

JAMIE

Natalie Fraser

Straight A student
captain of the soccer team.
A player collision: the result
a broken collarbone.
The doc prescribed opioids,
then upped the dose.
(Big Pharma claimed the drugs weren't addictive.)

The craving out of control. I saw him
slouched on the sidewalk, in a dirty
hoodie, a crumpled paper cup beside him
with a few coins in it.

At the funeral his mother wept.
Her son, her beloved son
taken from her by the money-lust
of they who laid her sorrow
on the altar of their greed.

SOCIAL JUSTICE

Binod Dawadi

You are hated you are discriminated,
You are bitten and scold,
Up to how many years,
You could bear the pains,
Up to how much time you will,
Hide your problems,
With fears,
You should have hopes and faith,

In self you are a strong and you,
Can do anything,
Speak for justice speak,
For freedom shout and cry,
Express your problems,
To your friends and relatives,
You should win the war of your life,
You should get your freedom one day.

ANOTHER TITLE FOR BOYS IN
THE CEMETERY

Abubakar Auwal

When mother grew her first tooth/ father was decade away from the age of men. // I ask if men can be gods/ or gods to be men/ maybe;// my mother would've cupped her grief/& named a peace behind the tears/ of the baby she gave to departure. // I versed this poem/ from the heart that sense the weight of grief// the heart that lost love at puerile days/ & the heart that was made from broken rhythm. // in another title this boy was fatherless, motherless & famililess/ like one buried on the heart of death. or the other one that find earth in the street of cockroach city.// & find himself caged,/ thought how to beg for bread/ from age-mate dressed to school/ or the other one calculating the formula in physics// or the other one searching for the laws in chemistry/ when sipping fire from the cup of flames.// this is another title for boys/ in the cemetery of dogs/ & here I prays/ father(s) should never again sold our future in the name of knowledge.

REROUTING

Andi Stout

Two years after the collapse,
exactly—a cantilever memorial
replaces the fallen suspension bridge,
connecting Ohio
and West Virginia once again.
Point Pleasant
High School marching band trumpets
an overture for a modest,
mostly local, audience
while the mayor cuts
a red ribbon with oversized scissors
signifying "open for business." A waitress

at one of the few diners left in town
serves coffee and bridge day specials.
Holiday bunting celebrating
inspection standards picks
at old wounds. She thinks about the look
of progress—15 missing
from the after-church rush,
Mother Jones and Paint Creek boys
in the mines, her brother
killed in Vietnam.

Why is it always at the expense of our own?
This is absolute, she knows,
like taxes and economic scars.

Dressed in their Sunday best
on a Monday, diners remember:
a sound like an airplane taking off
when chain suspension broke.
Volkswagens, Oldsmobiles,
semis, Fords, and Chevrolets
belly flopping like toy cars
into a 40-degree river rushing south.
concrete flipping like a pancake
done on one side then tumbling after—
the temperature dropping.

They talk about how the Silver Bridge...
...used to sway a little
under the weight of rush-hour
so much depending on an eye-bar.

YOU WILL HAVE TO COPE WITH
IT AS IF IT'S STANDARD OR
SUPERLATIVE

Ndaba Sibanda

ZESA, is there light at the end of the shaky shaft? A no-power utility. Son, you will have to put up with garbage, what else do you expect when you languish in a coo where lies are cooked, colored, cuddled as the truth, the one and only way to a dreamland of honey, not hell. Where hearths, bulbs and stoves are alien to heat, light or cooking. Where dimness is expediently mistaken for brightness and beauty. Where vain and foul fawns and clowns will defend the indefensible. They will convict anything, everything, everybody— nature included.

They will promote and praise either perpetually potholed roads, or projects that have been in limbo for literally forty-four years, and slam any sane soul who says it is good to be positive yet it is naïve to abruptly believe that a man who botched to notch up a tiring marathon race when he was young and strong— would superbly win it at the age of 44 or at a 'past' one. Where is the logic? If naivety were a soul, that soul would never ever see the light of redemption! Well, the Zimbabwe Electricity Supply Authority has gloomy news. ZESA has bared low and Lord-have-mercy scary load-shedding lists.

Tough luck, if you are not an adherent, a facilitator or a beneficiary of the system, but what else do you think when you live in a bubble where they do the same odd, old things over, yet expect unlike ends? You will have to put up with lousier, lengthier and harsher periods without power and peace. There is a solemn drought that is decreed and depicted by an acute shortage of water. Perhaps that one can be pardoned? However, the 44-year old drought of ideas and development, hell no. Its colors: decay, damage and corruption. What did you expect? Dear denizens, brace up for longer days of dryness, dreariness and denialism.

BEFRIEND THE PURPLE MAN

Melanie Flores

The black woman is your teacher.
The yellow boy is your neighbour.
The red transgender is your child.
The white lesbian is your grandmother.
The green queer is your friend.
The blue girl is your lover.
The purple man is the unknown factor.
Should you fear or marginalize
the purple man because he is unfamiliar?

We are all humans living on this planet -
so different from each other
yet so very much the same.
We all bleed, cry, live, love, laugh and die.
Revel in the uniqueness of individuals
and learn from them instead of judging.
Tolerating injustices makes you just as culpable
as the cowards who commit them.

Befriend the purple man.
Hug him when he's down.
Laugh with him when he's up.
The purple man could be

someone you know
- he could even be you.

A FOREST'S LAST WHISPER

Vanessa Caraveo

Orangutans, tigers, rhinos and elephants
may one day become lost in the abyss
for their habitats are being destroyed
by industrial and agricultural expansion.
Greed and power blinds men to their own evil
as they eradicate homes of innocent creatures
who cannot defend themselves against such villainy.
Will our grandchildren see these majestic animals?
Possibility looks dimmer as time goes on
for not enough is being done to stop such injustice.
With each tree that is timbered down
a forest animal becomes closer to becoming extinct.
Man fails to understand that Mother Earth
is home to all creatures and that only God rules.
I long for the day we can live in peace
and respect the homes of all beings in this planet.
For what good is power and money
if you have to destroy or kill to attain it?
Animals know and sense they are in danger
and will no longer have the forest to call their home.
Humankind from all over the world must unite
and stop such wrongdoing toward innocent beings.
How would we feel to lose our own homes?

We possess the power to make a positive impact
and must do the right thing and stop deforestation now!
Through the calamity the forest's last whisper is for justice
so her beautiful creatures may live in peace once and for all.

YOUR STATE CAN PROTECT YOU
FROM YOUR OWN CHOICES

Cecil Morris

Another law banning gender-affirming care
takes affect (in Texas this time), and I think
about Viagra and Cialis, which some might call
gender-arming care that restores the great sword
of manhood to men who have lost their edge.
Of course, those men are not minors, and they deserve
whatever help a doctor can provide to make
them feel good about themselves and their gender.
That is true for breast or buttock augmentations
for women who feel too straight or uncurvy
to receive the affirmations of their gender
that they desire, but not for minors, I suppose.
What about make-up, hair extensions, certain kinds
of clothes or weight-lifting regimes to build muscle?
Should the state begin to regulate those practices
if used by minors, with or without a parent's
consent? Texas could become the make-up state
and Florida the state that forbids bulked up boys
from competing with those who don't have weights.

EDGES

Agrimmeer DeMolay

it could be monday, could be friday, the sun blazing
on the hoods of cars pulling
into the department-store parking lot.
fresh through the automatic doors,
between dry wreathes and boxes of chocolates,
the bullet proof backpacks in the seasonal section
sell out, because it's better

to have every edge.
in the courtyard at the middle school,
hearing the clap of gunfire,
no one sees where it's coming from
—no one sees shit.
but many expected this, this, this,
to emerge in their lives one day,
and this is it.
one kid backs into a corner;
another dives under the table;
another jumps the fence;
now he's outside, running down an alley

hoping it ain't a dead end, thinking,
if only I had stayed home,

if only I went for the restroom,
if only I turned left back there.
in the foyer, another girl, another guy,
another kid, another, another, another
goes down,

like they're gripping the edges
of any solid thing during a hurricane,
some of them slipping
away into the wind, all
of the taken taken from those left holding on,

on what could be a monday or a friday.
with a final burst of sound, echoing
down the hallway,
the shooter ends himself,

body slumped against smooth
cinderblocks. on the other side
of the wall, in a classroom full
of disheveled desks,

nothing's heard
except varied ringtones
of cell phones, ringing,
ringing, ringing.

FOLLOW THE LEADER

Lynn White

It's so easy to be led,
to become part of the audience
seduced by powerful words,
by the performance
on the stage where
leaders make followers
not herded like sheep
but running,
with the crowd,
trying to keep up.

Individuals aren't allowed
in the crowd
and don't want to be there
don't want to become
an alternative leader
don't want to play that game.

And individuality
doesn't have the warm glow
of follow my leader,
the togetherness,
the comradeship,

the shouted slogans,
the rousing tunes,
the ceremony.
It's for the few,
the one offs,
the weird,
the misfits.

And where is the crowd
being led to?
It doesn't matter.
They'll go!

SHE

Adriana Rocha

She was given life,
she was given dreams,
she was given strength,
she was given a voice,
she also needs
the freedom to choose
whether to become
a parent or not.

JINTISHI POEM FOR THE PANDEMIC WINTERS

Marieta Maglas

White as snow, this hospital
still waits for doctors.
Feeling out of touch,
the nurses dance low

and button the jackets of the snowmen ~
gold and silver coins.
In their right hands ~ syringes.

Weave between contaminated strands
new hallucinogenic nights
with lives that are in crisis,
ill-fated weights.

Every weep-poor-will feels like hibernating.
Carry cars as conch shells
make yellow, black, and white spirals
to receive some hot news.

All ends up, getting the worst of it~
No chance at all.

Coils towards a faraway
And hidden dimension.

THE RED WINE SPARKLES AS GAMMADION BURNS

Joseph E. Arechavala

The red wine sparkles as it spills into the boot,
The boot that remains pure, pristine, its holy blankness
Prepared to crush crescents into golden nighttime moats of safety
    for kings and princes
The walls will protect us, high and safe from the dragons we write
    in Sanskrit blood
Blood that will redeem us as gammadion burns
ubiquitous glow of addiction
constant diversion
big-time entertainment
gladiators on the gridiron
bribery, scandals
adulterous exultation
oppressive odors
behind locked doors
blizzard shots ringing out
omnipresent victims
lying on floors
crying, bleeding
cut and gutted
from dynamic commercials

reality show hosts
despotic barons
just a touchscreen away
jingle jangle casinos
and campaign slogans
tent cities in December
festive in holiday lights
birds fall from the sky
flyover counties resentment
alabaster animus
unbalanced equilibrium
fake mountain springs flow
into muddy crass rivers
inventive sources
fabrication constellations
in a blackened sky

CASUALTIES

Dotty LeMieux

I'm talking to this woman I know,
but not in real life, just on Facebook,
about the Ukraine-Russia conflict.

We're talking of small children
in bombed out buildings. We're talking
about children who didn't make it out
before the bombs fell.

So many dead children—I say.
So many people with no home to go back to.
The mothers who wail.

Russian soldiers have mothers too—she says.
280,000 dead Russian soldiers.
If I could see her expression, I'm sure
it would be stern and emphatic.

I wait a minute, then an hour, then
I answer her:

But they are soldiers—I say,
not ordinary people.

They are—she says,
and their mothers mourn.

LAYOFF

Peter F. Crowley

We regret to inform you that you are being let go.

Your services are no longer needed. We have selected a team of skilled tech workers in the Philippines to do your work. If their country's wage goes up (which we are lobbying against), we will move operations to Laos or Mexico. Perhaps, AI may do your job soon; that's our ultimate goal. Algorithms cost nothing.

What's that? Yes, we know that those who develop AI are well paid and costly, but we'd only hire a handful of them. Once they create and maintain the algorithm, the majority of employees will be, how shall I say – poof!

Your work over 25 years was stellar, it's just that we prefer to cut the fat.

Why are you frowning? What do you think I'm implying – that you are fat? Oh God, no. We would never say such a thing. In fact, we have a DEI director who has implemented several trainings to ensure that our words are cleaned with Clorox and wrapped in cellophane, while embracing diversity. I used fat as a metaphor for the corporate body which, to survive, has to remain lean. You know: a real lean, mean, muscle machine! I joke.

Don't be glum; there is plenty of work out there. It may not be statistical analysis like with us here, but there are several industries that are begging for people to apply, like Starbucks, Uber and Stop & Shop. No, of course I don't mean long-term, just until you find something else.

What's that? Those kinds of places don't have benefits and you have type 2 diabetes? Well, frankly, that's not our problem. Your health is your own business. You were lucky that we subsidized your insurance when you were with us. Just pick yourself up by your bootstraps! Besides, we also offer four weeks of severance pay. That's pretty generous, if you ask me. Some argue too kind.

And, by the way, we're going to let you leave early today – little sign of appreciation from us. Thank you and best wishes.

NOT BURNT OUT YET!!!

Mohammad Haseen Ahmed

What a life if full of care!
Gone in vain in restless, snared
In the vain glory of daring acts
Only to remain captive intact
Not meant to be born to leave
Our mother earth parched and bare
Never thought a day would come
When we would scoff at each other
Unlike brothers and sisters, mother and father
Who we are after all, if not just the sheer chips of the same block
Why do we continue to inflict miseries of our own making?
Why don't we learn to live in fraternity?
Who the hell after all we are
To ravage this planet in our whims and fancy?
Don't we ever contemplate
Retrospect and realise how much destruction
Apathy, nonchalance and negligence
Aspire no more ,desire no more
What if, there is no redemption, no resurrection of the lord,
    Christ!!!
Wake up, grow up not in desperation
Jolt forward, don't look behind, it is scary
Tarry along and hope not to be the same again

THE CURSE

Anna Judit Hegedus

The forest feels.

There's blood EVERYWHERE! Where did all this come from? Oh, no!! I see my friend covered by his own gore. One of his arm is missing... It's lying not far from him. The blood is all over him... Wait... It's all over ME! I panic... Now that's a terrifying situation to wake up to.

"Jeez, what happened?" I'm asking while trying not to get a heart attack. The smell of blood is sickening. I don't know how we ended up here. It's like a blackout in my brain... a memory loss about the last hour or half an hour? Honestly I'm not even able to tell the time... I guess we went to the forest together with Paul to cut trees for firewood. But I can't find my saw anywhere. That's weird...

Paul doesn't get up.

I climb to him on my knees and shake his shoulder. Oh my God! His shoulder! I can't... Not this look! I step away and throw up my whole lunch (I don't even remember if I had lunch), but I can't help it...

Then I look around and realize that we're in the darkest and creepiest woods ever. The uncomfortableness of this frightening place can be felt really hard. My anxiety level is increasing... The unbelievable calmness and silence of the place scares me. It's like something, no wait, everything is looking at us. Frightening! What are we even doing here?!! The wind is freezing and around us there's a circle of dense fog I can't see through. As if the forest wanted to hide us. To keep us safe from something big. In the air evilness is drifting. "What the fuck?" - Paul wakes up.

"Where are we? John this is ridiculous, I can't feel my..."

Oh, no! He looks down slowly right where his arm used to be.

"What the fuck..." - his voice breaks. He opens his mouth to scream.

"A......"

"Shhhhh" - I put my blood covered hand on his mouth. "Some-one's gonna hear us" "Well at least someone's gonna help me!!"

Paul answers. "My arm..."

"Ohh..." I notice that the blood is still leaking from his shoulder. It looks awful! "Let me tie and fix it with my sweater." "FIX IT???!!! You know how far it is from fix?!"

"I do! I see! Just calm down you're not helping me by making so much noise!" "Not as if anyone would hear anything..." I can feel the pain in his sarcasm.

"And I'm sorry, but at least your body is still is one piece and mine's not even close to that condition, so what are you expecting,

... that I smile and say I'm good, let's go home from this... What is this place anyway?!"

"I told you to keep your voice down!" "I don't care what you..."

JUST SHUT THE FUCK UP!" - I shout without self control. It's too much... Way too much!

My words are echoing far in the woods. So far that if I weren't that dizzy I would believed that the trees are repeating that I just said.

"You heard this?" - I turn to Paul while looking up the gray cloudy sky and listening carefully.

"Look, I don't have time for your shit right now! We need to get out of here ASAP!!! "You're right. Any idea how? This is a complete labyrinth! Oh wait..." - I notice a lantern nearby. I ran to it and hopefully look for matches in my pocket. I try to light the lamp and... it's working! Now we have light! "Be careful...!" - Paul warns me while getting up but it's already too late. I stumble in a root sticking out, the lamp slips out of my hand and breaks into pieces. Our little source of light is gone. "Good job Jonathan!" - I murmur nervously. - "I swear this forest is fooling with us!"

"Yeah, could be true..." - I heard my friend's sight.

"Wait... where's Tom?" - Paul's face turns into pale.

"I... don't know..."

I was so shocked that I totally forgot about Paul's little brother, who came with us to the forest... We can't see him anywhere...

IF WE DO NOTHING

Rob Rolfe

(Part of *Gaza Poems*)

under the rubble
are books
and the bloody broken
barely formed

bodies of babies
and the quelled voices
of children
unable even to cry

and if we do nothing
there will be
blood too
on our own hands

THE RED-WHITE-RED FLAG

Natalie Fraser

A horse called freedom
galloped through the fields of Latvia
his sun-dappled coat blood-red
with a pure white band.

When the rope went round his neck
he struggled to break free
but the savage beatings stopped him
– submit or die.

Misery, toil and hunger,
winters of bitter cold
his only friend a brave young boy,
the servant of his cruel master.

Years passed, dreams of escape dimmed
skin and bone, coat faded –
until the paddock gate opened
run, the boy said, pointing west.

The horse charged through the gate
the red-white-red horse
untethered at last
the horse called freedom.

NIGHT SYNDROME

Emmanuel Umeji

She splashed on the bed. It's how he taught her of night—
to open out like a kneaded dough & wait until
something goes into her, into the wormhole between
her thighs. Nights after nights, the night
bears with her the weight of the jumbo brute on
her fragile bones. It piles all her snivels & yelps,
fold them into her blanket for her to scroll through
at daybreak. She awakes, finds the remains of the
night between Her thighs & tries to forget them in tears,
tries to wheel on her life, tries to spin herself
a white lie that her world is colourful, tries to keep
world's ears out of her pain. & when night comes
shutting her day behind doors, she melts into her usual grieve,
all spread out on bed, awaiting the advent of the brute,
who morphs her nights into a ritual of pain-tasting.
But pain is not the tempest thing that comes
into her as a stick; it's thinking about him pouring
into her loam, same seeds that forged her.

PILGRIM OF SURVIVAL

Abubakar Auwal

far, singing into broken night

my sister darted herself into broken syllables

of fire. i sing her

from the intoxicating heaven

beside her lips.

she's a dead butterfly, watering her ribs

into a journeying storm

of mud, of rain

& tears that gauge

the roses on her cheeks.

beside this poem, she lives

thousand times to plant her tooth

on the face of god, of you, of me

& the sermons of what you puzzled the earth with.

after this poem, i'm wrapped to dictate

the chuckles in her bones.

she's eye goddess to how the

exasperated boreholes burdened

with the anthem of pain that

sings me to rain the earth. justice earthquake.

a soul like her, equal yours. her laughter sized

the smile of your lord. i don't know if

you truly knows that we both

share the same wind. we breathe the gravity

of every physic our bones can solve

& let the theories pounced on the belly of wormhole.

mother victimized her fading dreams, too.

father murdered them. for sure she may blessed this poem

with the colors of her dream learning to find

cottage in between the walls that universe her lad

with the study of suicide as she boiled silence

from the pot that burnt down, the pilgrim of justice.

PLASTIC APPLICATOR

Andi Stout

Inside a laguna blue plastic applicator,
cotton too densely packed
never sits right in the body,
contorting and blooming—
its expansion pattern butterflying
all wrong. Still, I place discharged
discrete cylinders
into a metal sanitary napkin disposal
hanging on the public restroom wall.

Non-recyclable, I wonder where
these plastic applicators go
all dolled-up dyed laguna blue.

Probably out to sea to join trash island.
Maybe the ocean current, wind and waves
will ferry them back to
a continental shoreline
to be recovered by global companies
looking to maximize profits
under the pretext of innovation
and sustainability. Maybe
plastic applicators dyed laguna blue

discarded in metal sanitary napkin disposals
hanging on public restroom walls
will become innovative window treatments
adorning airy breakfast nooks
and extravagant solariums of the top 1%.
Or sleek and modern designer sunglasses
that don't compromise on style.
Maybe ammunitions manufacturers
looking to go
eco-friendly will produce
bulletproof vests kevlar infused.
Or maybe someday
they will become industry itself—
sprawling factories made of plastic
manufacturing plastic
for use in other plastic—
a turducken of plastic.
Plastic for plastic's sake.

SILENT WITNESS

Melanie Flores

The woes of the world
weigh heavily on my soul
I seek out the Moon -
For solace? Answers to the madness?
Waxing in peachy abundance
she shimmers in the April night
and crosses over to my side
as a woman, human in form,
effervescent in spirit.
We walk, and we talk.
She speaks of the horrors
she witnesses silently
from her place in the sky.
Every spot in the world has its
disasters – natural and manufactured,
massacres, lies, greed,
discrimination, and disease.
The soulless feed the hungry
on propaganda.

She sweeps her arm broadside,
opening a curtain on the horrors
she witnesses every night

war and greed and fear and hate –
the poison of humanity.
Amid the tumult, I spy a young girl
writing a letter of support to another girl
in a distant war-torn country.
"There's hope as long as
there are people like her."
says the Moon, returning
to her spot in the sky.

THE RETRACTION OF RIGHTS

Vanessa Caraveo

It only took hours, not days.
Just hours for conservative states
to start stripping rights away,
eagerly signing law after law.

Roe vs Wade was over and done.
We thought America had won,
that freedom and common sense
had conquered the day.
We assumed that the ruling
would be here to stay.

Where do we draw the line
between when the justices
can turn fast on their heels
and say a ruling never happened
and when the outcome is real?

Now the fight starts over again.
Decades of clawing up and out
torn down in an instant,
to the tune of lament.

Teenagers. Rape victims.
Mental patients in the ward.
Anyone can be pregnant
but the future we strive toward
gave them one last chance.

Now it's gone and the dawn
of a government ruled by superstition
and religion rears its ugly head.
Our souls will be trapped
wherever we're bred.

The bodies we thought we finally owned
have been stolen by a courtroom.
They are no longer our own.

MARY TELLS HOW IT WAS AND WILL EVER BE

Cecil Morris

Now, now don't you cry or feel embarrassed.
Let me tell you how it always starts. It's hard.
Jesus failed at his first drag show, honey—
that beard, that raggedy robe, those awful feet
in awful sandals—but he had the voice
and he learned by watching how others did.
He shaved and got some close-toed heels just high
enough, got one of us Marys to do
his make up and slick back that mess of hair.
Jesus was prettier than Joel Osteen
by the time us Marys was done with him.
We showed him how to move, was good to him.
Let me tell you that boy could sing, like you.
O that voice! Jesus, when he lifted it,
he made Etta cry at last and yell, "Yes,
sweet Jesus, sing!" That boy shined. He sparkled.
He reached right into your soul and took hold.
When he was on the street, you'd never know
what a special revelation he was.
Now don't you let them see you cry, honey.

Don't you let them stop you from turning heads,
from letting your song pour right out of you.

THE SIRENS OF THE PYLONS

Agrimmeer DeMolay

Their cement wall oozes with rivulets of run-off
that pass untranslatable scrawl
half-in the shadow of an underpass.
We again hear our footsteps,
between the south-bound bridge and the north—,

past a clothesline and an erect tent,
a lane of ground not owned
as much as it's lent,
denizens hidden by the rush and the roar of traffics.
One of them there spills morsels of her story,
sitting upon a pylon, palms upward.
She says she once dwelled
under a fine ceiling, was caught dealing,
and an eviction slip came.
She couldn't afford the baby, and so a sacrifice was made
before he could grow a name. "They tell you the gender
if you ask." Talk to the walkers,
among mold-blackened cement
and guardrails full of dents.
Under these same steel beams,
she'll do anything you ask,
for the right price. Learn as much as the length

of your stay, a little more to the story
with a tug on a sleeve.
The sirens of the pylons know more plies
than I could conceive.

No PCs, no gym memberships,
no credit cards, no course load,
no salary, no benefits, no ETFs, no Fendi,
no double-entend,
she goes without doctors—while forever on the mend.
Once she had all that, plus extra to lend.
She thought the army was her arc, a means to an end.
Bivouacked in Iraq, she'd be on an upward track,
but a boyfriend, court-martialed
for a stabbing in the back of the barracks,
sucked her in. Discharged and without a car,
where would she go? Anywhere could
end up being home. She's got time to list her grievances
over the roar of an expressway.
"Look around at these other faces,
two in December, ten in May."
She found a use for the discarded few,
"a crew that needs a revival and a tougher lead".
The sirens of the pylons know more of survival
than I would ever need.

ALL GONE

Lynn White

They built the roads.
They built the bridges,
the power lines and masts.
But still the landscape was empty,
deserted, lifeless, abandoned, hopeless.

And then they built fences.
They're good at that,
building fences
to keep THEM out,
not let THEM cross.
So still the landscape was empty,
deserted, lifeless, abandoned, hopeless.

As abandoned as an empty shopping trolley,
as abandoned as those who pushed it there
in desolate desperation.

And then it snowed.

SAME PLACE

Adriana Rocha

My house
Is your house,
My yard
Is your yard,
My park
Is your park,
We share
The same space,
Please help
Me keep it well,
Therefore, it can
Last for those
Who will need it
When we both are gone.

POEM FOR CHESS

Marieta Maglas

By integrating a completely new rule into
a new arrangement and having a completely
new tactic, the white king tries to drive
the antagonist king into the wrong corner.
He collaborates with the bishop.

The white king is quite rich. He takes
seemingly costless characteristics of individuals
and turns them into his property as he safeguards
the system in which they were enslaved and
still exploited. The population is blind and quite poor.

The black king has power and respects private
property and the right of the people to freely
obtain and use this property. However, the black
king is genuine. The bishop becomes greedy
since his two important cards are identical.

Furthermore, he can split the cards into two hands.
This way, he can play freely. He is trying to hide
since he is paid to do so. However, he can succeed
since chess is a sport that is gaining momentum.
It turns out that chess could be a simple game.

The last thing you should check before uploading or
downloading chess is if you know its secrets or
if there are certain relevant themes in the game.
The movement takes place in a real space and
sometimes includes equally real and fictional events.

There are twilight zones where you can play secretly,
but you must have an infinite number of ideas.
If you can fix something, you can rebuild it into
a whole new complex formula. If you are brave enough
to play with no limits, you can afford to play with no limits.

If you don't dare to play, do not play.
It is the same bleeding and quite not
breathable atmosphere in-between
cracks, active volcanoes, sinkholes, and tsunamis
for the same quiescent and dying earth for all.

THE RAIN FOR GAZA

Dotty LeMieux

Outside my window, rain
pelts down heavily,
wet, soaking,
delaying the daily dog walk,
which the waiting dog,
eyes pleading,
does not understand.

In Gaza, bombs rain
down drenchingly, reign
over the people,
soaked and forbidden
from going outside their borders.
Bound inside boundaries growing
ever smaller, tighter.

While on BBC television, the Israeli
Death Minister says:

> *They can leave. They got out of where*
> *they were before, they can leave.*

Knowing they have gone
as far as they can go, refugees

with no refuge, his eyes
cutting left,
cutting right,
staring a dare
straight into the camera.

The moderator blinks:

> *Well, we're
> out of time.*

On the floor, patient,
the dog sighs.

10 SECONDS TO LIVE

Anna Judit Hegedus

Once before you die
you get one last chance
when you can relive
your life,
your last few minutes
when you close your eyes.
Your soul calms down,
and your heart slows down,
your mind is falling asleep.
It's a final countdown,
or rather a cooldown,
before a completely new starting?
This game is confusing...

10 seconds to live...

I see myself being born...
my parents are crying.
These are tears of joy,
but they don't know nothing
about how I will disappoint 'em
I don't deserve them...

9 seconds till death...

I'm already a kid
playing around in the garden
with Suzy,
my only and favorite dog.
She passed away
and never returned
to make me smile again.
I was probably ten...

8 seconds to remember...

my teenage years
so memorable.
Yes, we were dumb and spontaneous.
We threw parties and got drunk,
after, we drove a cool truck
First love...
sweeter than ever,
like wind chimes
play a song so special.
We travelled a lot,
built sandcastles,
sent postcards to all the family members
We laughed: "That's all that matters!"

7 seconds to regret...

We grew up together
but things got bad
I was left behind
It was just me and I.
Only had my body

not my soul.
I felt empty chasing fun
I could never get back
So I drank
more and more
I wanted alcohol.
It wasn't me anymore,
just a doll...

6 seconds to rethink...

I found myself on the streets.
Sound of sirens
muffled in the distance.
I lost everything...

5 seconds to wait...

It's bitterly cold
I'm still breathing
but it gets harder and harder
to keep going
I don't know
how much time I have left
before I freeze to death.

4 seconds to forgive...

My tears are turning
on my cheeks into ice
It's too late for me...
I realise
that all I feel is weakness and cold.
I'm starving,

haven't eaten for days...
whatever...
It's over for me.

3 seconds for hope...

I slowly close my eyes,
I start to pray in my misery.
It's something I learned years ago

When I was a kid...
We sat at the table
I remember
with mum and dad...
we were grateful for
what we had...

2 seconds to pray...

"Dear God!
I know I'm helpless
I can't fix my life...
Still I'm begging you,
one last time,
please forgive me,
and send someone
who'd look after me.
Someone who'd kneel down
at my grave and say:
"I miss you"
My Lord, I'm hearing you calling
and I won't resist,
not now...
I have nothing to leave behind,

not even a normal life

I take the second chance
you're giving me...
hope it'll never end..."

One last second to say goodbye...

It's time to leave
I'm going home,
towards the sky!

IN THE NAME OF GOD

Melanie Flores

For too many decades, false gods,
hiding behind bibles and crosses,
stole the most precious treasures,
tearing families apart.
Thousands of priceless lives taken
in the name of segregation,
in the name of God.
Who were they to speak for God?

To drag children
screaming from their homes?
Murderers and marauders.
Heartless cowards.
Fearing what they didn't understand –
in the name of God.

They saw those eyes – innocent and vulnerable.
Instead of drying their tears and
giving them comfort
they denied them love and life
and laid their small, tortured bodies

in the cold and lonely darkness
to be swallowed by the earth.

If this could happen here,
it could happen anywhere.
In the name of God!

THE BOMB, NOT A BOMB, THE
A BOMB

Agrimmeer DeMolay

the a bomb, not a bomb, the a bomb
should be further than it is,
but it's so close.
we know how to make it.
what does that get us?
use the engine hoist to close the inner chassis,
like a giant easter egg of steel,
seal in the packed pu-239.
keep the geiger counter on
at
all
times.
remember, if you see a payload glow,
you're dead.
if only if only if only we didn't need this,
but we do, don't we?
the balance scale for the tnt charges,
protractor to get the spacing right,
a giant cloved orange of metal and mini bombs,
coordinate the detonations.
I would use a simple cpu to connect them,

to drive the detonator to ignite the tnt.
when is a weapon so deadly we need to call it
something else?
is this still a bomb, like with guy fawkes?
seal the outer seal. how do you
want to wire the switch?
can't stand next to it
when you switch it 'on'.
protect that button.
and decide where will
it
be
kept?
the a bomb, not a bomb, the a bomb
should be later than it is. but it's on time,
unfortunately, unfortunately
even for those who make it.
but we know it inside and out.
what does the knowing gain?

CONTRIBUTORS

Mohammad Haseen Ahmed, a distinguished research scholar, holds a prominent role as a lead presenter at the English Language Institute, KAU. He has chaired research collegium forums, moderated discussions, and participated as a panelist alongside globally renowned researchers.

Joseph E. Arechavala has been writing for over 20 years. On the autism spectrum, he hopes to contribute to awareness and engagement with the autistic community. He has had poems and stories published online and in print, and has published a novel, Darkness Persists.

Abubakar Auwal is an award winning author of Portrait Of gods As Metaphors; 1st runner up Nigeria Prize for Teen Authors (Poetry, 2024). He was the winner of Splendors of Dawn Poetry and Short Story Competition (February-April, 2023), finalist BPKW Poetry Contest, NYTH Poetry Contest, & longlist Brigitte Poirson Poetry Prize, shortlist Arting Arena Poetry Chapbook Contest and others. He's the Editor-In-Chief at New Voices Magazine, Founder/President of Nigerlites Spoken Word Artists as well as the librarian of Hill-Top Creative Arts Foundation.

Vanessa Caraveo is an award-winning bilingual author, published poet, and artist who has a passion for promoting inclusion, empowerment and equality for all, helping others discover the power they possess within themselves to overcome adversity and persevere in life. Her work brings focus to many social issues that exist in today's world and has been published in Literature Today Journal, The Poet Magazine, Latinidad Magazine, Poetrybay, Anacua Literary Arts Journal, and in multiple anthologies throughout the years.

Carol Caruso is a retired educator who enjoys writing. Throughout her career, she wrote newsletters and articles for her community and students. She has been published in Educational Leadership and is featured in Writer's Digest (March/April) as the winner of their "Your Story" contest.

As a prolific author from the Boston area, **Peter F. Crowley** writes in various forms, including short fiction, op-eds, poetry and academic essays. In 2020, his poetry book Those Who Hold Up the Earth was published by Kelsay Books and received impressive reviews by Kirkus Review, the New Age and two local Boston-area newspapers. His writing can be found in 34th Parallel, Pif Magazine, Galway Review, Digging the Fat, Adelaide's Short Story and Poetry Award anthologies (finalist in both) and The Opiate. His books That Night and Other Stories (CAAB Publishing) and Empire's End (Alien Buddha Press) were released during the week of Friday the 13th in October 2023.

Binod Dawadi, author of The Power of Words, holds a Master's degree in English Literature and is based in Kathmandu, Nepal. With over 1,000 anthology contributions, he aims to enlighten society through his writing. Binod is also deeply involved in digital photography and painting. His work has been showcased in prestigious exhibitions, including the International Art Festival in Korea in 2023. Combining literary excellence with visual artistry, Binod is dedicated to societal transformation through creativity.

Agrimmeer DeMolay grew up in the New Haven area and now resides in the Hudson Valley. Even though his backgrounds are in physics and housing development, he's been caught writing poetry more than once, as seen in Rhino, DoubleSpeak, and AntiPoetry Magazine.

Natalie Fraser writes poetry in English and Latvian. Her poems have been published in Poetry Pause, Latvija Amerikā, Chasing Sunsets (an anthology) and are forthcoming in Stray Words and confetti. Some of her poems have been set to music by composer Erika Yost and performed in concert; one will be performed by the Mass Choir at the 2024 Latvian Song Festival at Roy Thomson Hall in Toronto.

Melanie Flores is a Toronto-born writer, editor, and poet. Melanie's work has been described as provocative and evocative and has appeared online, in print journals, and in various international and national anthologies. A multiple award-winning poet and writer, Melanie is a member of the League of Canadian Poets, The Ontario Poetry Society, and The Writers' Union of Canada. Melanie was a judge in LCP's 2021 Jessamy Stursberg Poetry Contest. Her most recent publications include a poetry chapbook, "The She: An Exposé"(2019), and a YA novella, "Whisper of the Golden Feather: A Spirit-Animal Chronicle"(2021). Melanie has also ghost-written several memoirs, freelancing as a Senior Writer for Story Terrace. Melanie recently completed work on her new novel, When Worlds Collide, and Kahloesque: A Book of Poetry.

Barbara Anna Gaiardoni received two nominations for the Touchstone Award 2023, recognized on the Haiku Euro Top 100 list for 2023 and on The Mainichi's Haiku in English Best 2023. Her Japanese-style poems has published in 145 international journals. They are been translated on Japanese, Romanian, Arabic, Malayalam, Hindi, French, Chinese, Korean, Turkic and in Spanish languages. Co-author of haiga and shahai poetry with Andrea Vanacore, visionary photographer & videomaker with a long and varied experience. Barbara & Andrea alias gaia & vana are life partners in Verona City (Italy).

Nick Garlick is a writer of stories for children (Aunt Severe and the Dragons, Aunt Severe and the Toy Thieves, Storm Horse and De Zusjes Jennifer). Born in England, he became a Dutch citizen in 2019 and now lives in the Netherlands.

my name is **Anna**. I'm a poet and a writer mostly online. I live in Hungary as a student and I enjoy writing poems and short fiction stories in my free time. My inspiration has many sources. My hometown, my family, my pets, and our lives, because I have so much to be grateful for.

Andrew Hough is a published author, poet and playwright who lives on the Isle of Wight. He is married with two adult children and to date three grandchildren. A qualified Youth and Community worker he has had several letters published in national newspapers. He also writes plays, sketches and short stories along with brief ballads as well as tall tales for children.

Liam Kerry is a thinking enthusiast with a bad memory - writing helps him recall his daydreams. He works as a Model Maker when he's able, in between battles with bowel cancer. Writing poetry and flash fiction has helped him through many miserable experiences. An anthology of his creations will be available in 2024, intended as a boredom-buster to be kept in the bathroom for people with similar chronic illnesses.

H.S. Leigh Koonce is the founder of Ellerslie Books and serves as editor of three of its anthologies, The Cardinal Anthology, Sincere Dalliances, and Udolpho. He is the author of two books, Erebian Musings, a collection of prose poetry, short stories, and fragments, and Stories from the Ballot Box, a non-fiction book discussing the political history of Jefferson County, WV. Koonce also serves as the founder and organizing director of the Shepherdstown Book Festival. He resides in the same part of West Virginia where his family has lived since the late 18th century.

Allan Lake, originally from Saskatoon, Canada, has lived in Vancouver, Cape Breton, Ibiza, Tasmania, Melbourne and Sicily. He has won Elwood Poetry Prize, Lost Tower Publications (UK) Competition and Melbourne Spoken Word Poetry Fest. His latest chapbook of poems, "My Photos of Sicily", was published by Ginninderra Press. Such journals as The Hong Kong Review, Quadrant Mag, Cordite Poetry Rev, The American Writers Rev, Tokyo Poetry Journal, The Antigonish Rev, as well as New Philosopher and The Fabians Review have published his poems.

Dotty LeMieux has published five chapbooks, two during the pandemic: Henceforth I Ask Not Good Fortune in 2021, from Finishing Line Press and Viruses, Guns and War from Main Street Rag Press in 2023. She has appeared in numerous publications and has received one Best of the Net nomination. She lives in Northern California where she practices environmental law and helps elect progressive candidates to office.

Joseph Levens' fiction has appeared in Gettysburg Review, AGNI, Zone 3, Meridian, Cream City Review, and many other places. He has completed three short story collections and two linked novels, one of which has been adapted for the screen. He has made finalist in contests such as the Bakeless Prize, Autumn House Press, Black Lawrence Press, and Atticus Books, and has an MFA in Creative Writing from Stony Brook University. He is founder and editor of The Summerset Review, now celebrating its 22th anniversary.

The Oddville Press, Sybaritic Press, Prolific Press, Silver Birch Press, Lothlorien Poetry Journal, Dashboard Horus, Al-Khemia Poetica: A Women's Arts and Writing Journal, Southern Arizona Press, Journal of the Akita International Haiku Network, The Queer Gaze, PentaCat Press, Coin-Operated Press, Mayari Literature, Ardus Publications, and others published the poems of **Marieta Maglas** in anthologies like Near Kin: A Collection of Words and Art Inspired by Octavia Estelle Butler, The Oddville Press Summer 2018, Nancy

Drew Anthology: Writing and Art Featuring Everybody's Favorite Female Sleuth, A Midsummer Night's Dream, Three Line Poetry, Tanka Journal, and The Aquillrelle Wall of Poetry. The editor of The Aquillrelle Wall of Poetry, Yossi Faybish edited her poetry book, Cubic Words. She is a co-author for A Divine Madness: An Anthology of Modern Love Poetry, Enchanted- Love Poems and Abstract Art, The Auroras and Blossoms PoArtMo Anthology: 2020 Edition, and Women of One World.

After 37 years of teaching high school English, **Cecil Morris** has turned his attention to writing what he taught others to read and (he hopes) enjoy. He has poems appearing in Ekphrastic Review, Hole in the Head Review, Rust + Moth, Sugar House Review, Willawaw Journal, and elsewhere.

Prayerlife Nwosu is a graduate of Mass Communication from Federal Polytechnic Nekede Owerri. She is a young writer who is determined to change the world with poems. Her poems have appeared in various Poetry Anthologies, Websites and Magazines which include: Anthology in honor of Late Professor Jerry Agada, 11th Woman Scream anthology, Abhyuday "The Rising" International Magazine, The Pine Cone Review Magazine; Issue II, News Corner Media, Poemify Magazine; Issue III, Libretto Magazine; Issue 07, 6 th and 7 th Chinua Achebe poetry/essay Anthology with awards of outstanding entries, gisthub24.com, allpoetry.com, Upwrite Magazine, Nigerian book of Miscellaneous Insults, Ghostly Ghouls and Haunted Happenings Anthology, OPA Annual Anthology; Bridges to Tomorrow, Voices of Africa Anthology, Voices of Revolution Anthology, The Graveyard zine's fifth issue just to mention a few. She is currently the state Information Secretary of the Society of young Nigerian writers (SYNW) Imo state chapter.

Joie Ocampo is a 2nd-year BS Psychology student from the Philippines, and an aspiring author. Her works center on the topics of grief, identity, and the complexities of human relationships.

Through her stories, she advocates for mental health, rights of indigenous peoples and persons with disabilities, and universal human rights and equality.

Adriana Rocha was born in Bolivia. She is a psychologist who has been writing for five years and was published in three languages. She believes in the healing power of art, and she has found in poetry both a way of expression and reflection.

Rob Rolfe is the author of seven books of poetry, three chapbooks and a co-authored book of poetry and songs. His writing has been published in many Canadian literary journals, and in anthologies in Canada and the United States.

Baby Satpathy, the author of this article " Social Justice against Gender Discrimination", is a Post graduate in Science from Utkal University, belonging to State of Jagannath Dham in India. Former Under Secretary to Govt; Culture Dept. She is a Motivational speaker, Poet and Writer, woman activist, writings mostly based on woman issues and other related social issues.

Ndaba Sibanda is a three-time Pushcart Prize nominee and an author of thirty-one published books of different persuasions and genres.

Magnolia Silcox is a Schizophrenic bisexual twenty-one year old author from Vicksburg, Mississippi. Her hobbies include writing, sewing, and watching anime. In her free time she sews dolls for kids in hospitals and refugee camps. She is also into theater and acting in several different plays within her community theater guild. She lives with her parents, younger sister and two little brothers. She is also an animal lover with one bird and two cats. She enjoys writing about Schizophrenic and bisexual people just like her.

Andi Stout is an Appalachian writer and author of Pushcart-nominated, Tiny Horses Don't Get A Choice. Her work has appeared in Mulberry Literary, Variant Literature, The Aerial Perspective, Northern Appalachian Review, Fire Poetry, Still: The Journal, among others. Andi earned her MFA at West Virginia University and lives in Pennsylvania.

Irina Tall (Novikova) is an artist, graphic artist, illustrator. She graduated from the State Academy of Slavic Cultures with a degree in art, and also has a bachelor's degree in design. The first personal exhibition "My soul is like a wild hawk" (2002) was held in the museum of Maxim Bagdanovich. In her works, she raises themes of ecology, in 2005 she devoted a series of works to the Chernobyl disaster, draws on anti-war topics. The first big series she drew was The Red Book, dedicated to rare and endangered species of animals and birds. Writes fairy tales and poems, illustrates short stories. She draws various fantastic creatures: unicorns, animals with human faces, she especially likes the image of a man - a bird - Siren. In 2020, she took part in Poznań Art Week. Her work has been published in magazines: Gupsophila, Harpy Hybrid Review, Little Literary Living Room and others. In 2022, her short story was included in the collection "The 50 Best Short Stories", and her poem was published in the collection of poetry "The wonders of winter".

Born and raised in Sioux Lookout, Ontario, **John Tavares** is the son of Portuguese immigrants from Sao Miguel, Azores. Having graduated from arts and science at Humber College and journalism at Centennial College, he more recently earned a Specialized Honors BA in English Literature from York University. His short fiction has been featured in community newspapers and radio and published in a variety of print and online journals and magazines, in the US, Canada, and internationally. His many passions include journalism, literature, economics, photography, writing, and coffee, and he enjoys hiking and cycling.

Patricia Thrushart writes poetry and biographies from her home in the Pennsylvania Wilds. Her fifth and latest book of poems, Goddesses I Have Known, was put out by QPC Publishing with proceeds benefiting a local domestic violence shelter. Patricia's poems have been published in numerous journals. She is co-editor of the blog and anthology series for North/South Appalachia and co-founder of the group Poets Against Racism & Hate USA. In 2021 her work was chosen for an award-winning anthology of Ohio Appalachian voices, I Thought I Heard a Cardinal Sing. She's had poems included in the "Women of Appalachia Speaks" series. Her narrative non-fiction book, Cursed: The Life and Tragic Death of Marion Alsobrook Stahlman, was published in December 2021 by Adelaide Books.

Cathy LaForge Tonkin is an award-winning graphic designer and artist, who worked in that field for thirty years. She enjoys water-color painting, pottery and writing. She has written 3 previous books, 'Leave 'er Lay,' 'Kids on the Porch,' and 'Upside Down and Backwards' and many short stories. Cathy lives in Minnesota with her husband Gary.

Lynn White lives in north Wales. Her work is influenced by issues of social justice and events, places and people she has known or imagined. She is especially interested in exploring the boundaries of dream, fantasy and reality. She has been nominated for a Push-cart Prize, Best of the Net and a Rhysling Award.